Beyond the Red Line

Funny Shit That Happens in the Operating Room

August 15, 2023

Deanne Cricks

Certified Surgical Technologist

NEWMAN SPRINGS PUBLISHING
320 Broad Street
Red Bank, NJ 07701

First originally published by Newman Springs Publishing 2024

ISBN 979-8-89308-108-4 (Paperback)
ISBN 979-8-89308-109-1 (Digital)

Printed in the United States of America

To everyone who helped me gather these stories
and donated stories of their own

About me, I have been a certified surgical technologist (CST) for thirteen years, and I have seen, heard, and experienced some pretty awesome, funny, and heartbreaking times in the operating room and the emergency room. I will only be sharing the funny and bizarre stories in this book, as this is meant for entertainment, not heartbreak. I've also inserted some very often heard and used phrases, again just because they elicit a giggle (from me, because I'm basically a fourteen-year-old trapped in a fifty-two-year-old body).

As I began this journey to share some awesomely funny stories, as well as some other bizarre crap, I was not prepared to read the funniest stories I have ever heard.

If you do not know what the red line is, then this book might not be for you, but read it anyway; you will get a few laughs.

FYI, the red line is a literal red line painted on the floor to mark the entry point to the OR, where only patients and OR staff are to go beyond. You are required to wear the appropriate scrubs, shoe covers, and head covers to pass beyond this point.

If you do not work in the medical field, have no fear. There is a glossary of terms in the back of the book. I suggest reading that part first.

If you need to pee, do it now. On second thought, take the book with you; you may need reading material.

Welcome to the operating room! I have compiled stories from many different people who all work or have worked in the operating room, and these are the stories from those people, all of whom have agreed to share them without acknowledgment.

When something happened in our OR, we had one surgeon who would say, "*You can't make this shit up*." He was not wrong.

Disclaimer: No HIPAA violations were made in the making of this book. All names and exact locations were left out to protect patient privacy. Remember, any of these stories can happen to anyone.

Disclaimer: All submissions are as close to the original format as I could tolerate, without having an OCD aneurysm. I apologize for any grammar, punctuation, language, and emojis. I did fix some of the major grammar and punctuation issues. Some stories could be embellished or made up; there is no way to fact-check, so remember these stories are for entertainment purposes only, and enjoy.

CONTENTS

CHAPTER 1

LOOGIES

Extubation Loogie

As a wee tech at my first job out of school, I was standing next to a patient talking to the CRNA (anesthesia). I had pulled my mask down since we were done. I was in midsentence when he extubated the patient. The patient coughed, and a big loogie flew into my mouth. I ran to the scrub sink, spat, barfed in the trash can, and ran to the locker room to brush my teeth. When I was done, I went back to the room. They were all still in there and the CRNA was still laughing.

Trach Loogie

My friend and I are walking by an OR. We see the nurse by the door, yelling at us to come in. (She was a bitch.) So we come in to see that the patient is not asleep. He has a trach, and he starts coughing. So this nurse leaves us to stand next to this patient while she stands by the door, waiting on anesthesia. The patient practically sits up, coughs up a huge trach loogie! It's flying in the air… My friend and I see it spinning, and it lands on the nurse's eye! She then yells, "My eye!" And runs off 😩😩😩 Karma!

I Swallowed It

Had an HIV positive patient in the recovery room. He sits up in bed suddenly and coughs up a mucus plug that flew out and into the open mouth of the anesthesia tech. She *swallowed* it in her surprise and gags while saying "I swallowed it." The two other nurses standing there both threw up.

CHAPTER 2

UR-IN TROUBLE

Golden Shower

We were getting ready to do an artificial sphincter case, and the patient had received his spinal anesthesia. The patient was positioned in the stirrups, and the circulator was squatted down at the foot of the bed, wrangling the SCD hoses out of the way, when all of a sudden, the patient coughed. Remember why he was there? Yep, golden shower! We all about died when circulator said, "It's in my ear!"

I just remember the surgeon standing in the corner of the room, giggling and saying, "No problem," when the nurse said she had to go change her scrubs.

The best part of this was she was originally supposed to scrub the case and had asked me if I would switch with her, as urology was my service (we are both nurses). Hysterical!

Not a Hernia

Speaking of fluid shooting across the room, we were doing what the surgeon thought was an inguinal hernia repair. As he made the incision, fluid shot across the entire room and hit the nurse—it was actually a hydrocele. Oops!

"My Mascara!"

Sometimes in the operating room the surgical tech can feel ignored or not respected. This day was one of those days.

I was setting up for an ORIF of a tibia and fibula. It was decided we would repair both because of the size of the patient and how much weight the bones would need to bear, so I stayed scrubbed in, waiting for the rep pans that I needed to finish setting up, as the nurses were setting up the bed and the rest of the room. There were three male nurses, each changing the bed as they walked into the room, never consulting each other. I just watched as each one came in, changed it, and left; then the next would come in, change it, and leave; and then the third changed it yet again. I just giggled as the bed was changed four times before the patient was rolled into the room.

The patient, a male in excess of five hundred pounds, had been in a very serious vehicle accident and was already intubated.

To set the scene: there were four nurses, two surgeons, a PA, an FA, and two anesthesia personnel in the room, in addition to me and the rep. The three nurses, all guys, all of whom do not listen to any woman 99 percent of the time. The FA, also a guy who doesn't listen to women, unless he's flirting with them. The PA, a nice guy but pretty quiet. The only other female in the room was a nurse who is probably 5'1" tall and probably weighs 130 pounds on a heavy day. Still to this day, I am not sure why she was even there. Nice lady, just not a lot of help with a five-hundred-pounder, since his shin was bigger than her.

Everyone was bustling around the room trying to figure out how they were going to transfer this guy over to the fracture table. I piped up and said, "Why don't we use the hover mat?" After all, isn't this exactly the reason why we have it? One of the male nurses holds his hand up to me as if to stop me from talking—a pet peeve of mine! I promise you when I tell you, I am not quiet, so I know he is not the only one that heard me. They heard me and chose not to acknowledge. A few minutes later, they were still struggling, so I said it again, "Why don't we use the hover mat?"

Again, I was ignored, so I just stood there and guarded my table.

Twenty minutes or so goes by, and they finally have a plan. Everyone is going to grab a piece of the sheet he is on and lift him over to the fracture table. Right!

As I was watching this debacle play out and absolutely helpless to change anything, even if I had wanted to, I saw that the foley had not been picked up. I said very loudly, "Someone grab the foley." At this point, one of the male nurses turns to me and says, "We've got this," and holds his hand up to me showing me his palm again.

They continue to move the patient without grabbing the foley, so I said it again, "Someone grab the foley." No response at all. I said it a third time, and still there was no response, but I did get the hairy eyeball from the same male nurse as before.

What happened next can only be described as a golden shower circus. The foley got wrapped around the patient's foot, it tore free from the drain bag at the connection, thank God, and sprayed every single person holding the sheet. The surgeon yelled, "It's in my mouth." I heard someone say something about their ear, on the wall, the floor, and then I hear the tiny female nurse yell, "My mascara." I died that day. Best part, not one drop landed on me or my table.

Missed Me

While on a medical mission, I was assisting our urologist for the entire trip. Several times, when we had a hydrocele, as soon as he got to the puncture part, he would tilt it to spray me with the hydrocele juice. He got me the first time, then I would keep dodging it.

Well, my nurse, not the smartest or nicest person, contaminated my table three times in one procedure. So when I dodged and it hit her in the face, I did not feel bad and had a very hard time stifling my giggles. He pretended he didn't even see it happen. I loved that guy.

Masked Kisser

I was doing a urology case with one of my favorite doctors, who loves to say and do things to leave me speechless, such as grabbing me and giving me a noogie, then tossing me into the substerile room.

This particular day, he had me straddle him so I could hold onto a pressure bulb and squeeze it when he needed to see clearer. Why he did not just use a pressure bag, I will never know. I digress. I was giving him quite a lot of grief, as I always did. We had our normal back-and-forth banter going on when a nurse who did not normally work with us came to relieve our normal nurse for lunch. She seemed a little annoyed by our banter. When she came to change the fluid, he leaned forward and kissed me.

Of course, we were wearing masks, so all he really did was kiss the inside of his mask, but it sure shut me up. My eyes were probably as big as saucers as the entire room stopped. You could cut the tension with a knife. I suddenly burst out laughing, and the whole room erupted. We had to stop for a couple of minutes to compose ourselves.

Shoe Cover Headdress

First of all, I just want to say how much I love my urologists, they make the day go by so nicely, almost, no matter how bad the surgery goes.

During the height of COVID, the hair covers for men were on backorder. We had the crappy bouffant hair covers, but no caps.

So Dr. McSteamy (as he will henceforth be called, upon his request; you know who you are) decided to rebel against the system trying to make him wear this bouffant. He is a bit follicle challenged anyway, so it doesn't even make sense to wear a hair cover, so he would come in wearing a shoe cover on his head. This continued for about eighteen months.

The best part of this was that sometimes he would forget he was wearing it and go talk to the families. What I wouldn't give to have been a fly on the wall to hear the discussions that happened after he left them. Like were they concerned about the quality of care their loved ones just received? Did they think he was developmentally challenged? Did they maybe think he did not know he was wearing a shoe cover?

Give Him My Card

A few years ago, I got divorced. I know, I know, don't be sorry. It was a good thing.

Anyway, as I started my online dating debacle (is all I can classify it as), I found out that there is this thing that guys do now when starting a conversation with a female. Before they have even had a conversation about favorite colors or hobbies, they send a picture of their man parts. What is that all about? News flash to all of you that do this: no penis is pretty or pleasant to look at. They serve a purpose, and I am not saying anything further about that. So I was telling one of my favorite urologists about this disturbing revelation, and he began to laugh. I stood there, talking to the back of his head with my eyes, giving him my best exasperated look, to no avail. Finally, he turned to me, and with the straightest face, said to me, "I have the perfect solution for you." I thought he was going to say stop dating or something even more foolish. Instead, he said, "The next one that sends you a picture of their dick, just tell them that it's okay, you know someone who can fix that for them, and give them my name and office number." It was the perfect solution.

We both laughed really hard, and the nurse and CRNA, who could not hear our conversation, both looked at us very suspiciously.

CHAPTER 3

SHIT HAPPENS

Mount Vesuvius

We had an impaction with megacolon on a very obese man. The doctor was making a stoma, and it was a huge piece of intestine. The guy was full of gas (poor everybody). Anyway, the gas was erupting like Mount Vesuvius and sending poop cannonballs out of the stoma...*oomp, foomp, foomp*... Like a lot. Hard balls flinging across the room on the doctor's side...a terrible mess...I'm trying not to laugh.

You Nasty MF

During a very long procedure where the surgeon was wearing a headlight, the doc tells the circulator, "I have to shit, unplug me." Of course, everything stops as we all wait for him to come back.

He returns to the room and gets scrubbed back in. The circulator removes the plug for the light from the surgeon's back pocket and inserts it into the light box. As soon as he lets go of the cord, he sees a brown substance all over his hand. He states, "What the fuck?" and almost calls the doc a nasty MF. I'm shocked, he's shocked, the FA is shocked, and the doc is oblivious, because of course he can only see the small field the light of his headlight is showing, and he's looking into the wound, not at all our dumb asses, and all of the sudden the smell of burnt chocolate fills the room.

He had put a small candy bar in his back pocket, so that hot cord melted it. We all died.

Pink Eye

I had a patient on the Andrews table that prior to intubation was saying she was worried because she had an upset stomach. At the end of the case, while she was still bent over on the table, she started coughing. She shot diarrhea clear across the room and hit the wall as well as the RN's face—who ended up getting pink eye.

Ass Cancer

Farted during a lap chole once, and the surgeon thought he perfed the bowel. I never told him that I ripped ass. He later found out when someone told him. When asked why I didn't fess up, I asked if he would've admitted to something that smelled like ass cancer?

Tighty-Whities

I was on call with one of my ooollldddd docs. We had a distended colon, full open-belly, Bookwalter situation. He's milking the bowel, and you guessed it—it exploded. We were both covered in shit.

At the end of the case, this eightysomething-year-old man shimmies out of his scrub pants, pushes off his shoes, picks up the discarded items in a heap and walks out of the room in his tighty-whities without saying a word.

Shitballs

I was a newbie in a big open-belly bowel perf, and the surgeon kept handing me balls of poop, which I would chuck in the kick bucket throughout. When we were close to finishing, the surgeon asked for irrigation, washed out several times then went looking again. He proceeds to hand me a last rogue ball of poop, stating "Here's a leftover," which I again chucked in the kick bucket.

He stopped cold, stared at me, and asked what I'd just done, saying, "That was the left ovary."

The Shit

It's Dental Friday. The surgeon is a nice guy, very self-sufficient. Really only needs a retractor holder and a little help.

Patient comes in. She's a little weird all around and starts talking about how great the doctor is. "He's awesome! He's been my dentist since I was fourteen. Dr. — is the *shit*." Wow! Okay! I look at the doctor and say, "Did you know that?"

He just laughs.

FF doc is scrubbing in. He says, "Well, actually, I *am* the shit.'" Lol. We told him that needed to be his business logo. "Dr. —. Because I Am the Shit."

Code Brown

Okay. Laser case using smoke evacuator. Patient in lithotomy. Code brown. Everything sucked into the smoke evacuator.

Viagra and a Weazel Ball

I was about seven months pregnant when I remember getting called in around 8:00 p.m. on a Thursday night for a foreign body removal. I headed to the hospital knowing that this would become one of my most memorable cases.

The patient was high on meth when he took Viagra and decided to put a toy Weazel ball (they usually vibrate but the battery life had run out) up his rectum. He did this at 6:00 a.m. and waited to come to the ER until thirteen hours later when self-retrieval was not accomplished.

The doctor, an older grumpy surgeon with size 9 hands, had a black cloud and seemed to have always received the foreign bodies. He was notorious for looking around the room to find the person with the smallest hands to play "go fetch." I was not in the mood.

It's important to tell you that I had the nurse call in the GI tech, so we could do a look-see during and after the case. The GI tech was very helpful in retracting through the case and shared a laugh with me when the surgeon used his poopy gloves to adjust the headlamp.

After many failed attempts to grasp the hard plastic ball, the doctor decided to place two thirty-cubic-centimeter balloon Foley catheters past the foreign body, blow up the balloons, and pull backward, hoping there would be enough tension and that the catheters would release the seal in the colon to bring the ball with them. Quite the opposite happened. The balloons popped, and it sent this older surgeon flying into my back table, knocking it into the wall. Many instruments went flying onto the ground where the surgeon also ended up.

As I was trying to hold back my hysterics and thoughts of having to call the orthopedic surgeon in to fix the general surgeon's old hip, the GI tech was genuinely concerned and tried to help the surgeon up. At that point, the surgeon scolded him and said he needed to be left alone for a moment.

He sat on the ground for the better part of five minutes before he stood up and resumed trying to retrieve the foreign body. As he tried the balloon attempt again, he asked me to stand behind him in case he fell again. No way was my pregnant self going to get in the line of fire. The nurse was in and out so much trying to help us get different instruments, so our poor orderly stood behind him to make sure he didn't topple over again.

Hours passed, and we had tried just about everything, including baby forceps. I suggested putting a screw into the ball so we had something to grip onto, and that ended up not working. The doctor asked for the drill back and decided to drill clean through the plastic ball (scary moment having a drill in someone's rectum), and all you heard was a huge release of pressure, and the ball practically fell out.

Please Google what the product is so you can have an idea of what was in this man's butt.

I worked with the ENT doctors Friday morning, and I couldn't help but laugh as he placed his headlamp, hoping for his sake someone thoroughly cleaned it from the shit show the night before.

Buckets

We had an anterior hip. Our patient had been put to sleep, and we were transferring her to the Hana table. Our nurse, with secured boots in hand, lifts and starts moving her legs up and over the bars to where she was now in between her legs, lowering them. Just then, our pain-medication-riddled lady's bowels relaxed, and projectile poop launched straight at our nurse and didn't stop pouring. our poor nurse started screaming *"Buckets! I need buckets!"* She placed the boots in their holders and ran out of the room, stripping.

Not a Perf

While closing during a colectomy, the nurse went to the other side of the room to fart. It smelled, and the surgeon smelled it, announcing that he had to reopen the patient until the nurse had to admit that it was her fart that smelled. Needless to say, she was quite embarrassed.

"I Farted"

A friend/coworker was circulating. I went in to give her a ten-minute break, and she tells me, "Great! I'm dying to go to the bathroom. I just had to fart." So the next thing I told her very seriously: "Did you tell the team? 😐 'Cause you are not wearing a gown; you may have contaminated the room." Immediately her face went cherry; she just went straight to the surgeon and said, "I'm sooo sorry!

I farted! What should we do?" (She was new.) I didn't think the first thing she'd go announcing that to the others. 🐦 I guess I'm not that good of a friend.

CHAPTER 4

YOU CAN'T MAKE THIS SHIT UP!

Seven Cups of Blood

Sometimes, a story just finds you at the right time. Tonight was one of those times. I work the night shift, so I do see some fairly odd things on occasion, usually having to do with things people fell on that went up their butts or the AirPods that someone shoved into their penis. As I was sitting in the OR lounge writing my book, the charge nurse popped his head in and said we have a postpartum D&C coming up from the women's center, possible hysterectomy. The case was being pulled, and I was in the room, getting the room ready; anesthesia CRNA was also in the room getting ready. The charge nurse and the anesthesiologist are both popping in and out with tidbits of information.

This was a home birth gone wrong. The patient had a midwife that brought her in. The patient is brought up to the OR by two RNs from Labor and Delivery, accompanied by the surgeon. Once she was asleep, we got the whole story from the surgeon. First of all, this was the patient's ninth child; that baby should have shot out of there like a lawn dart. The midwife looked like she was ninety years old.

> Surgeon: Is there retained placenta?
> Midwife: There could be retained placenta.
> Surgeon: Has she lost a lot of blood?
> Midwife: Yes, about seven cups. [I shit you not,
>   this was her actual answer.]

Time-out time, and the anesthesia provider begins to list the patient's allergies. The surgeon pipes up, "Don't believe her. This chick is batshit crazy." At this point, the surgeon is standing between the patient's legs, and my nurse tells him he can do this any way he wants. I don't even know what he was referring to, but my doc does a circular motion with his arm around the whole area and says, "I don't want *any* of this." I laughed. A lot.

Human Bobblehead

This one time in the OR, I was working with an orthopedic surgeon who was known to have a short fuse, making everyone in the room pretty tense. So when something funny happened to him, we could not stop laughing. My circulator even peed her pants. Here's what happened during a total hip surgery.

First, I have to tell you that the surgeon and PA were wearing ortho hoods. The surgeon barks at the PA to dislocate the hip, so the PA has a bone hook around the femur head, pulling with all his might, when he comes flying off the femur, nailing the surgeon under the chin, knocking his helmet off his head. But because of the material from the hood that is still tucked tightly in his gown, the helmet does not fall to the floor.

So the surgeon starts yelling and swearing while trying to wiggle his helmet back on his head without using his hands. He turned himself into a human bobblehead! I laughed so hard I had tears running down my face into my mask. ☺

Skull Flap Down

One of our terror neurosurgeons, while bitching about the incompetence of our staff at this hospital and how the hospital across the street always has exactly what he needs when he needs it and knows all his preferences, dropped a part of the skull on the floor. Staring at the skull flap on the floor, he had nothing else to say.

Needless to say, he was much more approachable and friendly to us after that. Karma, bitch!

Questionable Fingers

Back in the day, everything was still written on a whiteboard. Not that long ago, to be honest. An anesthesia doctor was running the board and would just rewrite procedures when they were moved to a new room, with or without a new team, and erase the previous one. Sometimes, for the sake of saving time, the procedure would get written in as a much-abbreviated version of what was previously on the board.

The surgery had been posted as an I&D of a finger with the presence of pus. Not what it translated into. The anesthesia doctor moved the case to another room and abbreviated the case. I just happened to be standing at the nurse's desk and witnessed it.

I stood there for a moment with my mouth agape. He turned around to walk away and saw my face.

"What?" he said.

"*Uuum*, did you read what you just wrote?" I asked.

He turned and read it aloud, twice, before realizing that he had translated I&D of a finger with the presence of pus into "Pussy finger."

He ran to the board to erase it, but it was too late, too many people had heard and seen it. Laughter ensued, and I don't know if he ever lived it down.

Not a Republican

A patient waking up from anesthesia, looked at the resident and yelled "You voted for Trump" a few weeks before the 2016 election. He was ready for a full ad lib political debate.

Astroglide

I had an orthopedic surgeon ask for Astroglide instead of lube in the OR! I was the only one that knew what he was asking for, so I ran out of the room laughing to go get him some lube! The embarrassment on his face was priceless because he was a very serious asshole! 😅😅

Seriously

Some people are two broken hands away from unemployment.

Gravity Is Stronger in My Room

Everything I dropped on the floor that day, my heart partner taped to my back.

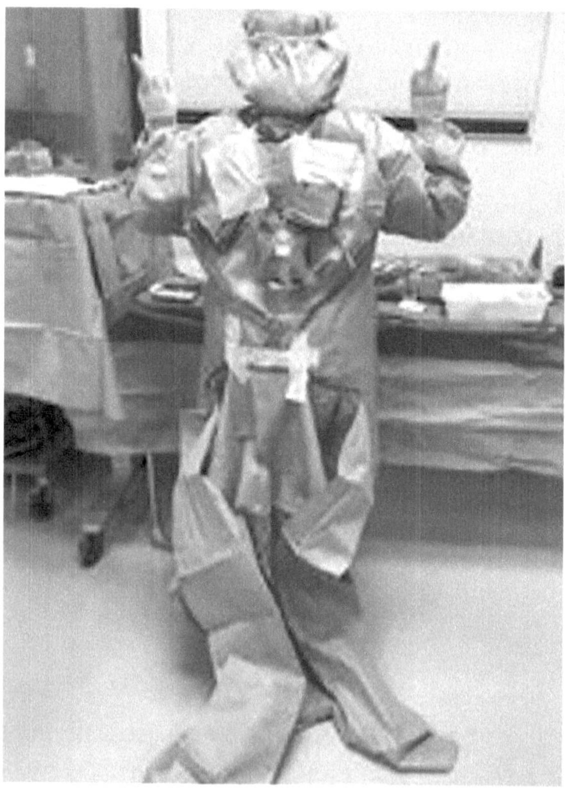

Cheese Sandwich

A PT (thirty years ago) in a small rural hospital was saving a cheese sandwich in her belly apron. Because after surgery she didn't want to have to wait for the doctor to put her back on solids. It also melted the cheese for her. True story!

The Bag by the Front Door

We had a patient's wife tell her husband to pack the "bag" by the front door for his surgery that day. (It had his shoulder brace in it.) Well, at the end of the surgery, the surgeon asks the circulator to grab the brace out of the bag. Circulator screams and says there is a raccoon in the bag. Of course, everyone thinks he's bullshitting at first. Well, there was, in fact, a taxidermy raccoon holding a beer can in the bag. There were also two bags sitting by the front door. One was supposed to go in the trash, the other was the brace. The moral of the story is to never trust your husband to do anything right. This happened to the funniest, most hardworking nurse I have ever had the pleasure of working with. He is happily retired, and I am so glad I recorded him telling that story in the breakroom because I smile every time it comes up in my memories. It was the funniest day I have ever had in the OR.

My husband has looked up all things to do
for when they bring down the gown, as to what
they will find.

Extended Warranty

One was a posted note in the belly button: "We have been trying to reach you about your extended car warranty."

Smoke Break

I came into the room to give a break at the end of a hand or arm case. We rolled the patient to get them back onto the stretcher, and a whole pack of cigarettes fell out of their gown. I tell people, the pocket used to be for cigarettes; I wish one of those people had been in the OR that day.

Didn't Recognize You with Clothes On

Came up to the hospital in street clothes for education stuff. Surgeon saw me from across the waiting room and screamed, "Girl, I almost didn't recognize you with clothes on!" I almost died.

*****

This happened to me too! A CRNA I worked with was quite the funny guy and saw me at the checkout line at the grocery store. We were about three checkouts apart; it was rush hour and busy. He yelled the same thing toward me. Everyone stopped, turned to look at my red face, then most of them laughed. A few of the older members of my church that were in line didn't seem to think it was quite that funny. I had to explain later why it was considered funny to me and my family!

*****

It happened to me in Walmart. Busy-ass Walmart, Christmas season, with my ten-year-old daughter with me. My orthopedic surgeon sees me from four checkouts away. He is 6'5" tall and yells, "D! I almost didn't recognize you with your clothes on. That guy you worked on last week is doing great." *Mortified!*

No Shoes, No Service

I had a physical therapist come to the OR to watch rods and screws in back, positioning, etc. She came in with the head nurse who introduced her, etc. She was a very nice young girl. After about two hours, she asked how long it took me to get used to the hard floors on my feet. I asked her what kind of shoes she was wearing. *She wasn't wearing shoes, just the blue booties!* I asked for a five-minute break so I could go down to the locker room with her. I wanted to laugh so hard, but I did not want to embarrass her. We went to the locker room, and she got her shoes.

Bic Pen

A twelve-year-old girl had what we thought was a lipoma on her scalp. Surgeon starts thinking what is this? He keeps dissecting. There is a little bit of pus, and out pops a tip of a pen. Cleaned it off with a ray-tec, and sure enough, it was the tip of a Bic ballpoint pen. The doctor said, "Well, I bet this will be an interesting conversation with the parents." How do you not know there was a pen stabbed into your head?

Her Package

Had a lady for anterior cervical fusion. When transferring her to the OR table, things were normal, except that the surgeon was catching the patients. When he reached across the hips to grab the safety belt, he got a little surprise boner against his arm. *Surprise!* Turns out she was a *he* who was identifying as a woman. The surgeon didn't know this until her "package" told him. Not a big deal for me, but quite a shock for him since the patient was still awake, and he had to play it off.

Pass Out

Man. You pass out while holding a penis *one time* in front of the whole OR, and you can never live it down.

WTF

Once had a sixteen-year-old female who swallowed twelve sewing needles.

and

My hubby had to help put a patient back on the OR table who had slid off during an inguinal hernia repair. All the while, the anesthesia was trying to reintubate, and surgeon was holding the bowels with a lap sponge. 😅 Also the patient was an inmate, and the guard watched the whole thing.

How'd that happen?

They think it was mostly the hover mat that was under PT and too small of a lap belt, so when they went head down and turned, the guy just slid right off into the anesthesia's lap. 😊

Expandable Foam

This guy comes into the ER complaining of pain in his penis. Turns out, he had injected expandable foam into his urethra. The excuse he gave was drugs. Ironically, the whole OR team was not satisfied with this. The surgeon tried to pull some out from the tip, but it was very stuck. They thought they could laser it until an RN said loudly "Doesn't expandable foam burn?" Google search later—yes, it does. They ended up having to do a cut down the shaft to pull it out and stitch it back up. 😊😊😊

These people give us job security, I swear. 😊😊😊

Can't fix stupid.

Nope, but you sure can sedate it. 😊

Sweet Potato

Elderly woman came in with complaints of "vines growing from my verginny." Apparently, she had a uterine prolapse and grabbed the nearest thing to prop up her uterus. Unfortunately, it was a sweet potato…that had sprouted. Removal by OR team. If I'm lyin, I'm dyin.

Apparently, according to one of the gyn docs here, the sweet potato was the most "ergonomic and readily available pessary in the Midwest."

I guess it worked until it sprouted.

In the '70s and '80s, we would have women come in who would use a pessary uterine prolapse (especially a sweet potato) until it didn't help anymore.

House Arrest

Working at a surgery center at the time. Young woman arrived for lap chole. Usual questions, anything to eat since midnight? Any medications since midnight? Smoke anything since midnight? Any metal in your body? Any jewelry or piercings. No, no, no to all questions. Pre-op staff get her ready. CRNA does their interview, same questions, replies the same. Circulator does interview, verifies same answers to questions. Consents are good to go. Patient is eager to proceed because she is miserable.

Arrive to OR, float nurse assists with getting patient moved over from stretcher. Goes to attach SCDs, notices they are not on. Hmm, rather odd they are missing. Lo and behold, there is a house arrest bracelet around her right ankle. Just about that time, the charge nurse comes into the room letting the staff know that the sheriff's deputies are in the lobby looking for this patient because the house arrest bracket had alerted. She was no longer at the specified approved location and was considered AWOL.

Patient started crying because she wanted the surgery since the pain was significant. Surgeon canceled the case because the deputies were not allowed to remove the house arrest bracelet without a judge's order.

An Elaborate Ring

Back when I was still circulating, I had asked a patient if all metal and piercings were removed, Patient states yes. Mind you, she's having a gyn procedure. The patient is intubated, we are putting her in stirrups, and what do we find? Her elaborate clitoris ring. Sweety, there's no way you forgot it was there, and why did you think we weren't going to find it? If you're not too embarrassed to let someone pierce you down there, you shouldn't be too embarrassed to tell your circulator.

Same situation, but they had barbell piercings in the back of their neck 😬 we didn't know until intubation.

Eyebrow Tweezers

We had a patient in the cysto room, she had been having repeated urinary infections, the doctor thought she might have a stone. We put the scope up and saw a very unusual-shaped stone. Upon further examination, we saw that it was a pair of eyebrow tweezers in her bladder! We did get them out, but we're wondering how they got in!

Mummy Toe

Put PT up in lithotomy for a cysto case. Noticed an odor from his foot. Removed his sock and found a shriveled, gangrenous baby toe taped back on. Put the sock back on. Let the urologist know. Documented findings and moved on.

Immaculate Infection

Long time ago, a teen came in for rip-roaring PID. Dirty-looking boyfriend to boot. Her mother was determined she couldn't have an STD because she had never had sex. I called it the "immaculate infection."

Diamonds Are a Boy's Best Friend

We had a patient with a foreign body in his bladder. Prior to going to sleep, patient begged us to save it, because it was his wife's bracelet, and she didn't know what he'd done. There it was on X-ray: a nice diamond bracelet, neatly coiled in his bladder.

The Burning Bush

Once I was assisting a GYN with a laser conization of the cervix. We had the patient draped with wet towels and the requisite wet 4 × 4 in the rectum. While we were doing the procedure, there was a very acrid scent of burning hair. The surgeon had inadvertently burnt a bit of pubic hair. A bit of fanning and some suction with the smoke evacuator quickly dispelled the smell. The patient was not burned. The surgeon continued working away. He muttered, "That was close!"

Our male circulator asked if he still had his shoes on. The doc glanced up and asked him why he wanted to know. He replied, "I thought you might have slipped them off since you were in the presence of the burning bush!" It took him a minute, but when it sank in, he could not stop laughing.

The Clamped Penis

When I was in scrub tech school, my preceptor towel clamped a penis to the drapes during an inguinal hernia procedure. We did not know it at the time, so when we ripped the drapes off, the towel clip ripped the skin off the shaft of his penis.

Not Singing in the Rain

About a year ago we did an aorta bifem that was rather lengthy and difficult. Afterward, the patient went to the ICU and was tucked in for the night. We all went home before the big snowstorm arrived.

Around 10:00 that night, I got a call from the surgeon saying we were bringing the patient back for a fem-tib bypass because the patient's family member, who is a nurse and works in management at the hospital, was insistent that his leg gets fixed at the same time. Also, there is like a foot of snow on the ground by now, and that is a lot for this area!

We return to the OR, same crew as earlier. We all happened to be on call to do the fem-tib bypass. In the middle of the case, water starts running out of the ceiling, and I feel it on the back of my legs. I'm literally the shield between the water and the operative field. We had to move the OR table out of the range of the OR lights to avoid the water. Luckily, our surgeon was wearing a headlight. It seemed like the water was our sign that we had no business being there, but we didn't exactly have a choice. It's a thousand wonders that the patient never got an SSI!

The Daily News

As a nursing student, came in to massage the fundus of lady who *just* had a baby. I was already nervous and not wanting to cause her any more pain. Walk into her and her husband tangled up under the covers, and they had covered the bassinet (with baby inside) with the daily newspaper.

Blow on This

This nursing student was scrubbed in, and we were putting in a Salem drain. It had a filter that had an airflow system that was not working. He jokingly handed the tube to the student and told her to blow in it. She literally pulled her mask down to blow in it. (It was already bloody.) WTF was she thinking?

What Window?

I walked into the equipment room one day midmorning, and the window was gone. Literally *gone*! Apparently, no one bothered to tell the department that they were going to replace the window that day. Who TF replaces windows? The building was only around seven years old at the time.

Truth Hurts

New OR nurse was asking the anesthesiologist why he had made a ramp out of blankets for this patient but not the others we'd had that day.

> Anesthesia: Well, when the patient is obese like
>   this, it helps with intubation.
> Nurse: Oh, I see.
> Patient: (still awake) Umm. Are you saying I'm fat?
> Everyone: 😶😳😬 (tension)
> Anesthesia: Yes… I'm sorry… (pushes the
>   propofol)

We laughed for, like, ten minutes once the patient was asleep. Like wheezing and cackling and almost peeing ourselves.

Prep the C-Arm

When I was a new tech just out of school, there was a new nurse also training in the OR. We were all draped throwing off cords, and the doctor said "Prep the C-arm." We're busy working, and next thing, we look over and see the nurse "prepping" the C-arm (with chloraprep)! 😅😆😂

Still to this day the C-arm is stained with prep stripes of orange.

Flagpole in a Hurricane

We had a midteenaged boy come in for a cysto look-see, and his parents wanted sedation. My circulator was the epitome of Nurse Ratched. (I loved her…mean old thing! lol) And trust me, she was *old* old. So anesthesia gives him a little dose, and the circulator comes over with the prep kit. Now you *know* you can't touch a teenager's peen without a huge reaction, and it was waving around like a flagpole in a hurricane. She was trying not to touch it, her face red as a beet. It was waving around, bamming into her hand, him giggling under the mask. I was crying. lol

"Can Someone Answer My Phone?"

Another time, we were finishing up a cysto case and had just moved the patient to the stretcher when my hospital Spectralink phone on my hip started ringing. The patient sat up and held his hand to his face like he was holding a phone and groggily mumbled, "Hello?" Everyone died laughing. Thank the Lord for Versed and the patient's amnesia.

My Hip Hurts

A little backstory: a guy comes to the ER with a gunshot wound to the abdomen. Evidently, he was fighting with his wife at 4:00 a.m., and she calls the cops. The cops show up, and the guy is wielding a gun. So the cops shoot him in the stomach. The bullet goes into the stomach and turns before even getting past the fascia and lodges in his hip.

So they roll him into the OR, and he is complaining that he is in so much pain and he is thirsty. We just keep working and ask if he can move over to the OR table.

> Patient: My hip hurts so bad, and it's getting worse.
>
> Me (in my head): Do you think it could perhaps be the bullet that is lodged in your hip?
>
> Patient: How can you tell when someone is drunk?
>
> Me (also in my head): Quite frankly, it's when they act like you, sir.
>
> Patient: Can I call my wife?
>
> Anesthesia: No, you are in the OR.
>
> Patient: I need to tell her that I love her.
>
> Anesthesia: No.
>
> Patient (agitated with anesthesia): *What's your name?*
>
> Anesthesia: Richard.

His name is not Richard, but told me he did not want this guy coming back and murdering him.

Meth and Chainsaws

A guy comes in with his lower leg chewed up from a chainsaw.

Patient states, "I wouldn't even have come in if that woman hadn't been there." No idea whom he is referring to.

Anesthesia asks him, "Have you been doing any drugs, sir?"

Patient says, "Yeah, I did some meth around six. Versed is beautiful."

FYI, that woman was his wife.

Surgery, Not Time Travel

I once had a facelift patient come back to the OR with a picture of herself twenty years younger so the surgeon could have a guide on what she wanted to look like. 😃

Two Big Thighs

At one hospital I worked with a really little OB-GYN. We had a patient come back to the OR with heavy vaginal bleeding from a previous procedure. She was enormous. I mean really enormous. We got her on the table and in stirrups, and anesthesia got her arms onto the arm boards with extra restraints on both to hold her in place.

The surgeon insists that light sedation will be enough. She's all prepped and draped, and the surgeon is standing between her legs. He swabs out the vagina and goes in with a cautery. He gives her one zap, and all hell breaks loose.

In one fell swoop, she rips the arm boards off the table and slams her legs together with the stirrups still attached. The surgeon, who is really little, is trapped between her legs. All I can see are his arms in the air and the top of his hat. A muffled voice is yelling "Help me! Help me!" We are frantically trying to pry her legs apart and hold her arms down so anesthesia can get control. Finally, she is down for the count, and we rescue the surgeon. His eyes were like saucers, and he just kept mumbling "What happened? What happened?" We were laughing so hard I thought I'd wet my pants.

I will never get the sight of his arms and hands flapping frantically between those two big thighs. The poor dude was traumatized.

What Prosthetic?

Fractured penis, and the doc had to remove his prosthetic. Speaking to the wife after the doctor relays the bad news that he had to remove it and was unable to put it back. "What prosthetic?" she asks. They'd been married seven years.

Unwelcome Lizard

During the construction phase of our OR in Houston, we had several suites that were not yet finished or finished but not cleaned up and set up for surgery, so no one really went into those rooms.

My circulating nurse (who I worked with most of the time) and I were instructed to go move some things from the room and get it ready to be set up. As my nurse moved a piece of equipment, a small gecko shot out and landed on her arm.

It's very hard to describe the shrieking chaos that ensued, as she is deathly afraid of all reptiles. She jumped straight up and backward at the same time, falling to the ground, her arms flailing. Her glasses that I thought had been around her neck on a chain but could have been perched on top of her head were now flying through the air with the poor traumatized lizard. She is now no longer shrieking, but still screaming. I am on the floor, laughing so hard I can't control the flow. I peed myself. There was no way to help her. This sent her into a chain of expletives that I cannot put in order, so I won't try, but the jist was she was really mad about me laughing at her misfortune, which made me laugh more.

After rescuing the poor little creature (who surely has PTSD from the incident) into a specimen container and depositing it outside, she (my nurse) finally realized the hilarity of the situation that had transpired and joined me in the uncontrollable laughter. For years after that, I would tape plastic lizards to her locker and place them inside to fall out when she opened it. She was not amused, but I always found it hilarious.

Why Don't We Get Drunk and Screw?

My friend and I were working with a general surgeon who only listened to classical music. During a bowel resection, I quietly asked my friend to put some Jimmy Buffet on instead of classical. I figured the doc was concentrating on the case and teaching the new resident. Well after five or six songs, the doc suddenly looked over his glasses at me and said, "Why don't we get drunk and screw?"

My friend and I just about wet our pants from laughing so hard.

Blow Job

I was working with a foot and ankle specialist, and he was a very prim-and-proper-type gentleman. You don't swear, you keep talk rated PG, and music on classic rock from the '70s. It was an ankle fusion, and the patient was under general anesthesia. He had a sinus infection going, and he had blown his nose before scrubbing in. He was sniffing and sniffing, with some coughing from drainage, and some deep sniffing as he was working. There was no real reprieve, and you could hear each time he sniffed that he needed to blow his nose in the worst way. And after he had been doing this for probably a good half hour and the patient was doing fine, I went, "Oh, my goodness, you need to get a blow job or something?" The scrub tech just burst out laughing; she was crying. She had to break scrub because she was laughing so hard.

The PA who was helping him was laughing and bracing himself on the patient. The doctor was just stunned, he went, between sniffs, "The gold medal goes to you for best comment and knocking it out of the park."

The surgeon broke scrub and went and blew his nose. When he came back, the scrub was back, and she continued to snicker, but the surgeon said he got the hint and took some sinus medication. The sniffing wasn't nearly as bad.

Centipede

Not sure if it's considered funny or creepy. But a standout moment was when we were putting a patient to sleep, and her last statement (as she was sobbing because she was scared) was "Don't turn me into the human centipede!" We all looked at each other wondering if we heard her right.

Then when we were done, as she was waking up, her first statement was, "I'm not a human centipede, right?!"

Sweetheart

I was in my clinicals, so still *very* new to the OR. I was working with a general surgeon that is always serious, also very impatient and crabby. We were doing a sentinel node biopsy, and the RN forgot to plug in the machine—he started stomping his feet like a two-year-old.

During the beginning of the next case, which was an open belly, I was turned, looking at my back table when he said, "Sweetheart—"

I absentmindedly said, "Yes?"

He said, "The retractor, I want the retractor."

I was mortified. Haha!

The Bug Book

Way back in the early '90s, we had a book at the OR desk. It was called the bug book. When we found a bug in the OR, we would squish it and take it to the bug book. We would scotch tape the bug in the book and write where we found it. ♡♡♡

Workout Partner

One day while doing a procedure, my surgeon, a woman who had twins a few years previously began talking about her new work-out routine that she had started. While we were all supportive, I mistakenly and very naively was particularly interested in what exercises she would be incorporating into this routine. "You should join me" she says sweetly.

> Me: Are you saying I'm fat, Dr. D.?
> Doctor: It's okay, you just had a baby.
> Me (adopted my daughter, haven't given birth to a child in eighteen years, staring at her in shock): I adopted K.
> Doctor (long pause): No way to fix this. You should join me.

Everyone in the room bursting into tears.

> Circulator (a man with many talents, gift-giving not one of them, solemnly says quietly): My wife said she was going to start working out last month. I bought her some work-out clothes for Christmas. I haven't had sex since. I don't think I'm ever going to again.

Everyone in the room laughing even harder.

"Cut It Out, Mark"

Had a patient midcolonoscopy look back at the doctor and say, "Cut it out, Mark, get off." (Mark was her husband.) 💀

Baby Momma's New Boyfriend

TN—had a guy who worked in a fish-processing business. Stepped on a catfish barb, pierced bottom of foot. He came in for I&D. He didn't follow instructions post-op—went to a demolition derby, got in a fight with his baby mommas' new boyfriend, and his dressing was torn off and foot dragged through mud. Came back multiple times and finally ended up with AKA. I wish I could share his name, because it is absolutely the icing on the cake.

Sugary

One July evening, the surgeon I was working with paged one of the new interns asking if they wanted to assist on a fairly simple case. The intern *ran* from the floor, put OR scrubs over his other scrubs, and came into the room, panting. Without a word, he power walked over to the whiteboard and wrote his name. Normally, it would say "Steve, PGY-1," or "Steve—Resident" or something like that (not his real name). Instead, he ham-fisted the marker and attempted to scribble "Steve—Surgery." In his flustered state, however, he misspelled "surgery" and wrote "STEVE—SUGARY." He then power walked out of the room to scrub in. He came in, soaked on his front half, and was confused as to why we didn't have a gown or gloves for him yet. My guy, you haven't even introduced yourself, I don't pick gloves for people I don't know… Well, Steve Sugary, if you could tell the circulator your sizes and ask real nice, maybe she will pull them for you.

Grab It Like It Owes You Money

One day, while working with a student nurse who was very young and very inexperienced in life, I had to witness her trying to put a foley in to a gentleman in his eighties. She was being so gentle and sweet, it was almost endearing. About five minutes goes by, and the penis has eluded capture for about the twenty-fifth time. The surgeon looks at me, rolls his eyes, and says "For fuck's sake, M! Just grab it like it owes you money." I almost peed my pants.

Item Received in Damaged Condition

Once had a patient for a repeat rectal procedure. The patient was a postal worker. As they were drifting off to sleep, they stated, "I hope you all have a sense of humor."

As we positioned them in jackknife, a sticker became visible: "Item received in damaged condition." Laughter ensued.

Here's my funny story. I thought I wanted
to be an OR nurse. I was wrong. (Anonymous)

I Got Your Mask

An anesthesia resident's mask and pants both came untied, and he didn't know what to do. I'm like, "Grab your pants. I got your mask." The resulting visual looked like I was hitting it from behind while holding his hair, as the charge nurse walked through the door and asked, "WTF is happening in here?"

Stripper

At one of our local clinical sites a medical student walked into a room with a cover jacket all snapped up. The CST told him to go out and scrub, but to remember to remove his jacket first. He walked back into the room after scrubbing with nothing on from the waist up!

Runaway

One of my students was observing in a very quiet OR when she let out a big fart. Everyone heard it and she got so embarrassed she quickly ran out of the room. 😄

Pants on the Floor

When I was a young, naive OR RN circulator, the surgeon's scrub pants fell down to the floor. He didn't step away from the field but expected me to right the situation. Picture this young nurse working his pants back up to his waist and retying them at the front waist, all the while maintaining sterile technique with my head and arms underneath his surgical gown. The old OR nurse I became would have done things differently, but back in the early 1970s I didn't dare dispute the doctor's "order."

Another time, during a very long and complicated lap chole, my pants had come untied and after trying to stand with my knees apart to hold them up, I had finally reached muscle failure and let them fall.

After finishing the case, the Dr. had stepped back and was stretching his back, when he looked down and saw my pants. He then looked at me and said "are those your pants?." Me, being a smartass, looked back at him and said, "Nope."

Fart Machine

Before I prepped a patient for back surgery, I placed a fart machine under the Wilson frame. After the patient was draped and the NP was marking the back, I started making the patient "fart." I laughed till I cried watching the NP jump back and swear up a storm.

Slippery Boob

While I was assisting in a mastectomy, which I always did, the Dr. went to hand the breast off to me. This breast was massive and super slippery from all the melted fat. That breast hit my gloves and kept on running—*flop*! It made the biggest splat when it hit the floor. I was mortified. Both me and the doctor just stood there looking down at it. I almost cried, until she burst out laughing. Thank God it was the prophylactic side.

Purple Cock Froster

As I was smearing bacitracin on the newly circumcised penis, the urologist said, "It's just like frosting a cake." There is a joke in my family that I'm the worst cake froster ever, so I meant to say "I've never been a good cake froster." Instead, I said "I've never been a good cock froster." I turned purple that day.

Spine Puss

I went in to give a break for a nurse who was doing a spine I&D. She had just collected a culture and was giving me report. I looked down at the paper, and she had written "Spine puss," instead of *pus*. I started laughing and pointed it out to her. She laughed so hard her face turned purple! It was so funny, I left it and sent it to micro that way.

Wrong Rep

Our scrub was setting up for a fracture case without rep pans for a new surgeon. This was his first case. The rep was late, and she didn't have any of the rep pans. The new surgeon entered the OR, and she started yelling at him that he was late and she didn't have any of his pans. The surgeon said he'd go get the stuff.

When he came back with it, the scrub angrily said to him that this is a new surgeon that she hasn't worked with and he, as the rep, was making her look bad because he was late getting her his stuff. The surgeon then said to her that he was in fact the new surgeon, not the rep.

By the Balls

My cardiac surgeon was the chief of cardiac surgery. He went to sit down in a stool to take the mammary down, and he missed his chair. I was behind him and caught him—by the balls. He quite literally looked up at me and said "Thanks."

Sometime later, he muttered something about his wife hasn't even touched him that way and that he may possibly owe me dinner. I mean I'll take a free meal.

Giddy Up

Today while doing a total knee, I accidentally kicked my attending on the ankle while attempting to shift my weight because my legs and feet were hurting from standing. He turned to me and asked why I kicked him.

I said, "I thought it would work."

He said, "What would work?"

I said, "If I kicked you, you would go faster, just like riding a horse."

He laughed so hard.

Wobbly Stool

Funny but not funny: I was scrubbing an ENT case sitting on a stool. The stool was a little wobbly, but I still sat on it. All of a sudden, the stool disintegrated, I fell backward, and while trying not to fall, I grabbed my back table and pulled everything off the table onto the floor, on top of myself. It made so much noise staff came running from everywhere. I just sat there, wet with saline-soaked scrubs and underwear. Doctor looked at me and said, "Go take a break. Be back in ten minutes." I was so embarrassed I just said "Okay" and left the room.

Moral to this story is "Don't ever sit on wobbly stools."

What Are You Doing under There?

I'm a PACU nurse, and occasionally we will help in the OR. (Usually with getting the first case of the day going, holding an arm/leg for prepping ortho, tying up a doc/scrub, on call, etc.)

Picture this: ENT case. Doc needed his headlight plugged in and asked me (the PACU nurse).

Having recently helped ortho (where the doc's helmet has a cord running down their back under the gown that then gets plugged into a light source), I walk behind the ENT doc, squat down, and lift under the back of the gown carefully and start blindly patting up the back of his leg, searching for the light cord. The doc pauses, turns his head around, looks down at me (basically under his gown with one arm, like I'm caught red handed with my hand in the cookie jar) and says, while laughing, "Uh. Can I help you?"

I freeze and reply, "I'm looking for your light cord to plug you in."

He points to his headlamp, "It's up here."

Everyone busts out laughing. And that, my friends, is how I almost died.

Before he retired, our running joke was asking me to come to the OR just to help plug in the light cord.

How Do You Tie Your Shoes?

Knee Scope / ACL. The surgeon, scoping and shaving at this point, says "Give me the bone cutter." Mind you, we're not open at this point.

Me (in my head): WTF is he going to do with this?"

I hand him a double-action bone cutter.

The surgeon stands there with it in his hand and looking at me like "How do you tie your shoes by yourself?"

It's a type of shaver by the way.

No Scrubs for You

I worked at a children's hospital where we did not have an ED, so we only worked the day shift, and you stayed till the case was over. We had a problem with our scrubs missing, so at the end of the day, they were locked up. On one long ortho case, we were putting on a cast when the attending, whose scrubs were very bloody, went to change. Scrubs were locked, so he came into the OR with just a lab coat on. He was very tall! Quite a picture. The nurse in the room looked at him and, without missing a beat, reminded him he did not have shoe covers on!

Don't Touch My Boobs

Older woman came in for a pacemaker insert, heavy MAC, Throughout the case she kept saying "Don't touch my boobs." Her husband had recently passed. She used the insurance money to have new ones installed.

Help Yourself

I was early in my career working at a teaching hospital with an endless rotation of new surgical residents and medical students. We had a patient in jackknife position for a hemorrhoidectomy, cheeks taped and prepped, when he proceeded to have projectile diarrhea that shot across the room and all over the cabinet behind him. The new resident turned to me while I was conferring with the scrub tech and said, "You gonna clean that up?" I told him where the towels were and that he could help himself.

Ron Jeremy

Ortho surgeon that calls the rongeur "Ron Jeremy."
First time I was like, "Excuse me?"
He appreciated that I got it and said it was too much explaining for some people.
#iykyk If you don't, I'm sorry I'm not sorry, for what Google might show you.
FYI, it's the *big* rongeur.

Nut Allergy

Had a surgeon tell me to make sure I pull the testicles back down after an inguinal hernia, told him, "Sorry I can't, I'm allergic to nuts."

Rubber Band

While pumping a CABG case, my assistant went up to help anesthesia hang a unit of blood. Before hanging the unit, he took off the rubber band holding the unit information. He hung the unit and, while fiddling with the rubber band, it went flying and landed right on the patient's heart! All you heard in a big roaring voice was "*What the f——k is this!*"

Penis Puppet

Was doing an inguinal hernia, got patient back and to sleep and took off the gown to prep and there was a puppet on his penis giving us a great big hello.

Using Your Head

Had a surgeon (he was new, maybe met him twice before)—he asked if he could use my head. Me thinking he was going to ask a question or for help in some way, I said no problem. He then leaned toward me and scratched his nose on my head.

I Need Fifty Bucks

We had a heart surgeon that some people didn't like working with. As we were about to go to sleep with our patient in another room for a different surgeon, one of the scrubs opens the door (thinking our patient was asleep) and shouts, "I'll give fifty bucks to whoever will come do this heart over here."

Our patient smoothly says, "Hell, I need fifty bucks. I'll go do it."

Open-Gowned Nakedness

Patient enters the OR, undecided if he really wanted to go thru with procedure or not; all staff were getting things ready, doing what they do, not exactly sure the sequence of events, as he was talking to others. All I know is when I turned around, all I saw was opened-gown nakedness running out the surgical room. ☺ What a sight to see! ☺

Birthday Suit

Wheeling a patient into surgery, and she tells me to stop in front of the operating room. She wants to walk into the OR. She had refused Versed in preop, so completely sober lol. She proceeds to take off her gown and throw it back on the stretcher and walks in with only her birthday suit ☺

Fifty-Five Long Years

Also, a sweet elderly man going back for a discectomy had Versed on board. He was kissing his wife as we rolled out of preop. As I'm wheeling him to the OR, I ask how long they have been married. He says, "Fifty-five years, fifty-five looonggg years." He then starts crying and says, "I've been faithful for fifty-five years. Do you know how hard that is?!" I was so uncomfortable lol. I thought he was going to say something sweet.

Charcoal doesn't ☻ bleed. Bovie the sh!t out of it!

Do You Think He Meant to Kill Me?

Had a patient who was caught by her husband cheating was shot multiple times (not seriously). Before going to sleep she asked if we thought he meant to kill her. Seriously?

Never Been with a Squirter

Had a GYN scrub get thrown into a total joint room way back in the day. We used to put plastic shields around the clean air zone that hung just beyond the sterile table, creating the zone of cleanliness. She was a good scrub but truly not in her element under the hood and in the zone. They were close to closing, so she volunteered to go in. They asked for the pulse lavage gun to irrigate. She snatched it up quickly and activated the lock on the trigger. It was blowing saline all over everyone as she looked for a safe place to aim it. All the shields were dripping. All the doctors and residents were dripping and getting splashed. She was whooping the whole time, "Oh! Oh! Oh!"

When the resident finally wrangled it from her, the doctor stated he had never been with a squirter before. Everyone busted up.

Pranked

Had a nurse that had a problem with figuring out how to prep for a lower body lift and tummy tuck. Not her normal service, so she spread a sterile sheet on the floor. Had the patient stand buck naked as she proceeded to paint her shoulders to toes, front and back in betadine.

The doc walks in to see the patient standing there, spread-eagle on a blue drape in a puddle of brown liquid while the nurse is on her knees painting her crotch like Van Gogh in short, stabby strokes. He lost his mind. He thought he was being pranked.

New to the OR

Oh my. So I'm completely new to the OR but not a new RN, so prepping is something I had not done before on a regular basis, and there have been many days where I've felt totally lost (still do a lot; it's a process). Reading this, I feel so much better now.

Asshole

One of my favorite surgeons walked into the OR, and I was scrubbed in, waiting for him to go wash his hands. He stands there looking around and pats the pocket of his scrubs looking perplexed. So I asked him, "Did you lose something?" and he said he can't find his glasses. I asked him if the ones on his face would work, he called me an asshole, and I smiled.

You're Going to See My Ass

A patient comes in for a colonoscopy, I introduce myself and tell him we will take good care of him. While waiting, I make some small talk, asking him a question, and he says, "I'm afraid you're going to see my ass."

To which I reply, "Oh don't worry, when you've seen as many as I have, they all start to look the same."

He says back to me *loudly* and *slowly*, "I can't hear you because of your *mask*." Oh my gosh, did we all laugh! Basically, most of my funny OR situations are rooted in me not hearing what's *really* being said.

Stop the Drip

So this girl was charging, but she had to do the case. A patient came in with a penny nail in his penis. When she asked him why, he said the medicine man on the reservation told him to heat up a nail and shove it in there to stop a drip.

Disappearing Screws

I have a story from when I was new to spine surgery. I was doing a TLIF, and it was an extension of a previous TLIF. The doc

I was with started talking to his PA about "disappearing screws," so we didn't need to remove any old screws. I thought it was weird, so I was asking if they had fancy screws that could dissolve or something. I wanted to know how they could disappear! The ST I was learning from just backed them up on it. I was so convinced it was a real thing until I googled it after the case! Almost two years later, and it still gets brought up. I'll never live it down.

Thermos

Found a Coleman thermos lid in the sphincter!

Pull Harder

When I was a student surgical tech (23 years ago) rotating through GU specialty, I was scrubbed for a prostatectomy. The surgeon placed a Penrose drain for retraction, and I was holding it. After a time, he told me to pull on the drain, and I cautiously did. He said, "You must really retract on it," so I did. The drain came flying out of the incision, and I just stood there panicking with a Penrose drain and this person's body part hanging from it. I didn't even know what to do. I just stood there for what felt like an eternity. But there was probably thirty seconds with the entire team staring at me like "What did you do?" Cue hysterical laughter from the entire room. I'll never forget that as long as I live. That is what feeling completely petrified is. I didn't realize at the time that it was the prostate and thought I just accidentally ripped something out of this poor patient. Thankfully, I just laughed too and had a great experience.

Dr. M's Vagina

Once, while doing my "time out," I said, "Our surgeon is Dr. M's vagina is our site," lol. No comma inserted, and the surgeon chuckled and said, "No, my vagina is not our site." We still laugh about this. As a matter of fact, we worked together today, and we had to tell the resident our story. Since then, I have changed the order of my time outs.

Stool

I asked a surgeon before a procto if he needed his stool pushed in when he asked for a pump-up chair.

Carrot

Evening case, exploratory laparotomy for foreign body removal (inserted rectally). When time came to remove the *huge* carrot, I was asked to take some pictures. On a step stool I go. "Everyone say 'Carrot.'"

Just the Tip

I was a baby circulator, and it was one of my first nights of buddy call. Spouse cut off the tip/head of his penis. Guess he showed her. Picture a twenty-two-year-old scrubbing the tip while her preceptor was scrubbing the patient. All I remember thinking is that my Catholic mother would die if she knew what her new college grad daughter was doing at 4:00 a.m.

Pee Faster

Okay, here is this one for the urology team! The patient is using the restroom for a urine specimen. The nurse tells me to wait outside the door for the elderly lady. So I wait and wait *and wait...* Then I'm like, *Okay, let me see on the chart what the patient's name is so that*

I may address and call out to her to see what's taking so long. Well, here goes... "Mrs. Pee-fister, are you okay in there? Oh, Mrs. Pee-fister, are you okay?"

She said, "*What!* What! I'm peeing *as fast as I can!*"

"No, ma'am, I'm not rushing you to pee faster!'"

She said, "You said 'Pee faster.'"

"No, ma'am, I was calling your name..."

"*My name is* Pfister*!* The *P* is silent."

And she had hearing aids

Wild Geese

Surgeon sent the new tech observing in the room for the left-handed lead hand and the Otis elevator. They missed the whole case on a wild goose chase.

Surgeon sent the student looking for left-shoulder scissors. She sweated for a while searching then he burst out laughing. The funniest part was when she laughed and called him mean and said, "You remind me of my papaw. He makes jokes like that." I then burst out laughing and called him Dr. Papaw the rest of the case.

I had a circulator once who was not a very "intelligent" individual. Let's just say English is not her first language. She just happened to be our hall facilitator that day and kept popping in to ask stupid questions. So on an instance when she came in, I decided to use my powers for evil instead of for good. Not proud, just stating fact! She came in, and I asked her to hurry and go get the keys to the channel locks from SPD in a rushed tone, like it was imperative that she find them quickly. I did not see her again. *All day!* It was fantastic. Again, not proud, but not sorry either.

Noah's Lights

During a total knee, patient had a spinal. He was very talkative and was asking some questions—very distracting, so the surgeon gave CRNA the sign to "shut the patient up." Once we were closing, someone started telling jokes.

Suddenly, the patient starts yelling "Hey, hey, hey!"

CRNA asks what's wrong.

He says, "What kind of lights did Noah have?" Bewilderment from the room.

She asks him again what's wrong; he repeats the question.

"Um, I don't know," she said.

Patient laughs and says, "Flood lights!" Then falls back asleep!

Everyone busted out laughing! Also, a reminder that sedated patients can hear what's going on!

Just Go with It

Prepped for cataract surgery, seventy-nine-year-old lady says she's getting dizzy. The CRNA told her to close her eyes and just go with it, she said, "That's exactly what my husband said on our honeymoon!!" We died!

You're Just Choking

Anesthesia waking up a patient: "Ma'am, relax, calm down. Ma'am, calm down, you're just choking." Lol

Slow as Shit

A couple of years ago, I needed to have my gallbladder removed.

A little bit of a backstory tangent: we work in a hospital that is quite religious (LDS).

I had an appointment for the following week to have it done.

I was working with a particularly *slow* surgeon whose tires I have since threatened to slash if he cut out suture for a third time. Anyway, we are chatting about the upcoming lap chole for me, and he offers to do it for me. I could not make eye contact because we were standing next to each other, as I was holding a camera for him. I just instinctively answered, "No thanks, I don't want to die of old age on the table."

He responded with a resounding, "Fuck you!" Now, no one heard any of the conversation at that point, so they had no context. This resulted in three other people in the room standing silent with their mouths agape.

We both laughed.

Gonorrhea

Sometimes, you can't really remember how a conversation started, but you can certainly remember how it ended. This was one of those times.

The discussion was about sexually transmitted diseases.

Anyone who works in the OR knows that anesthesia does not always know what is happening on the other side of the drape.

Well, gonorrhea was the topic at this point, and our CRNA pops up from behind the drape and says, "I had that. It was terrible."

Now, not one of us knew what to say, so we just fell silent. Finally, the doctor looks up at him and says something to the effect of, that was personal and too honest.

> CRNA: Everyone has!
> Doctor: Nope!
> CRNA: If you've been swimming here, you've
>   had it, whether you had symptoms or not.
> Doctor: *What?*
> CRNA: It's in all of the water supplies here.
> Doctor: Are you talking about giardia?
> CRNA: Yeah, what are you talking about?

We all laughed so hard we had to stop operating for about five minutes.

Flasher

We were getting ready to sandwich flip an A/P spine patient. Halfway through the flip, the Jackson arm board bracket caught my scrub top, and as we continued to flip the patient, it continued to lift my scrub top up. I yelled "Oh my god!" which is not really what you want to hear mid-sandwich flip. Everyone denies seeing anything, but I know they are just trying to be nice.

Popcorn

We are waiting to do an open prostate in the lounge munching on snacks, about one hour into the surgery, a piece of popcorn pops out of the surgeon's mask and into the open wound. We all just froze. He quietly picked it out with a forcep and asked for some antibiotic irrigation. Nothing more was said about it. A usually talkative surgeon said nothing the rest of the case.

The Elusive Snickers Bug

While on a mission in Guatemala, we were doing a hysterectomy, and the assistant, a very old, retired surgeon who always assists, even in the States, kept blowing into his mask. About the third or fourth time I heard him do it, I looked up at him and asked him if everything was okay.

His eyes got big, presumably because the realization that this could be a bug in his mask that keeps tickling his face. Then he burst out of the OR, forcing us all to run to the window, ripped his mask off, and threw it to the floor. He began stomping on the mask like a madman.

Calmer now, he picked the mask up and turned it over. Nestled neatly inside the mask was a tiny Snickers wrapper. He must have dropped it into his mask between cases.

At the final dinner, he was voted most likely to mistake a candy wrapper as a bug. It was rehashed every single trip after that. I loved that guy, even he laughed about it.

Nice Boobs

So in the military, we do a lot of gynecomastia surgeries, and I was scrubbed in, and the patient was being prepped. His man boobs were pretty small, and my intrusive thoughts manifested into words, and I said, "Wow, he's got some nice boobs." Everyone in the room stopped and stared at me. I whipped around pretty fast to find something to do on my back table and turned bright red. All I could think was, *Damn it, that was my outside voice. I wonder how long it will take HR to call me.* We laughed about it months later.

Surprise Sort of Proposal

I am anesthesia, and I was waking the patient up. The patient wakes up and says, "You are not my wife." I told him no, but he'd be seeing her in a couple of minutes. He then asks, "If I get a divorce, would you *be* my wife?"

Popping Her Cherry

Had an elderly patient who fell and broke her hip. Scheduled for a gamma nail, as we were shelling her back to the OR, she said that she has never had surgery in her entire life, had kids but no surgeries. Proceeded to say "so you're popping my cherry."

I'm Not Even Sorry

I came to work one evening and was told I had a laparoscopic case to do with a surgeon who is not incredibly popular at our facility. Someone else had opened and set up my case, so I waited to scrub in until the patient was in the room.

When the surgeon came in, he told me that he had told the charge nurse he would not need another assistant since I was with him. I got him gowned and gloved before it dawned on me, so I asked him, "Did you say something nice about me?"

To which he replied, "Yeah, I guess I did."

I was pretty shocked, since we have a relationship where we constantly flip each other as much crap as humanly possible. So I asked him if he had taken his meds that day. He said he must have forgotten, obviously.

He uses cysto tubing and a suction irrigation tip that is not on the battery-operated suction irrigator. He likes to throw off his own cords so that he can have everything just so; he's on the spectrum, so he is very particular. I was bringing my table up when he starts to yell about his feet getting wet. I look over, and the cysto tubing is not clamped, and the nurse has spiked the bag. He is still in a frenzy and trying to clamp the tubing. I look over the patient at the puddle that has formed around his feet, and I look at him. While I am laughing, I say, "I'm not even sorry." He finally laughed as well.

Surprise Penis

Over twenty years ago, I was getting ready to prep/put a Foley on a hernia patient who was labeled as a female. After pulling back covers, I noted a penis instead of a vajayjay. Surgeon stopped in his tracks. "No Foley for this case." Totally mortified, he didn't even know about the gender change. I assumed he didn't even do an exam presurgery either! Good thing, Times have changed now. Listed all over the chart!

Cheese Sandwich

Had a patient (thirty years ago) in a small rural hospital, who was saving a cheese sandwich in her belly apron. Because after surgery, she didn't want to have to wait for the doctor to put her back on solids. It also melted the cheese for her. True story!

Question: Was it at least in a zip lock?

Nope!

No Smoking in the Hospital

Patient waking up from anesthesia "smoking" their pulse oximeter. Nurse tells them there is no smoking in the hospital. "Oh! Sorry." And the patient attempts to Flick their "cigarette pulse ox" out over the edge of the bed! Lol

Groped

There was a surgeon wearing green scrubs standing beside the anesthesia machine after the patient was extubated. The scrubs we wore were the exact color of the bag on the anesthesia machine. The patient was having laryngospasms, so the CRNA was doing positive pressure to break the laryngospasm. She knew where her machine was positioned so she would reach for the bag. Out of the corner of her eye, all she could see was green. She didn't realize the surgeon was standing there, and she was reaching for his crotch and didn't realize it. That really helped the tense situation in the room, and the patient did okay too.

Farted

I rolled a patient into the OR one time, and as soon as we go through the door, she says "I just farted. Is it still sterile in here?"

Bunionectomy

We could hear the patient coming in through the automatic doors. Monitors beeping and lines running everywhere. The patient was intubated. Someone said, "This must be Dr. G's bunionectomy."

Good Soldier

I have worked in the OR for over twenty-five years, so I have a few good stories, but here is one I will always remember. I was a scrub tech working in a military hospital. We had a male patient wake up pretty aggressively, kicking and yelling. We tried to calm the patient down with no success until the CRNA says in a strong, deep voice, "Attention, soldier!" The patient snapped to attention on the OR bed with a sharp salute, pulling the arm board off the table. He saluted with the arm board still strapped to his arm while yelling "Yes, sir!"

Watermelon Sugar

I was in the OR yesterday with two very Mormon surgeons. Every nurse in the room and anesthesiologist is wearing crucifixes, and I'm sitting there holding a retractor. "Watermelon Sugar" comes on, and I'm vibing, living my best heathen life. Then one of the surgeons stops and looks up at me and says, "What does it mean? What does 'Watermelon Sugar' mean?" and I said, "No. No, that's for you to go into incognito mode and look up later."

He said, "Oh come on, just tell me. It's something sexual, isn't it?" and I said, "Sure is." I will not, *no*.

Three verses go by, and he's like "Just tell me."

I said, "*It's the female orgasm*," and a hush fell over the room.

Nobody said a word for at least a minute and a half.

Resident heathen strikes again! Don't ask questions you don't want to know the answer to.

Get It Out

I was first assisting on a lap chole with one of my favorite surgeons. As we were pulling a rather large stone-filled gallbladder out of the umbilicus, the endo bag broke. He and I were grappling with Kelleys to get the gallbladder out, and—*pop!*—out it came. It actually went flying in slow motion into the air, smacked me on my forehead, slid down the inside of my face shield, and nestled itself perfectly across the bridge of my nose. I just stood there with my eyes closed, repeating "Get it out! Get it out!"

You know when people are laughing so hard, and no air is actually coming out? Well, that was the *entire room*. Everyone was deliriously laughing so hard it took them at least five minutes to fish it out and clean my face.

After that, I could never first assist a lap chole with that surgeon without him breaking out into hysterics.

Sorry, I Drink

Doing a lap chole with a surgeon who has a history of being irritable at all times, and he's just opening above the belly button for the trocar, and I had been working with another surgeon who always used scalpel, Kocher, Kocher, scissors. So he asks for a hemostat, and I hand him Kocher. He drops it and asks again for a hemostat. I hand him another Kocher because obviously something was wrong with the first one. He looks up at me and says super slow and kind of loud, "*Hemostat.*" I was so embarrassed, I just looked at him and said, "Sorry, I drink." He busted up, and he was never irritable with me again.

Krazy Glue

I came to the operating room fresh out of nursing school with no prior OR exposure other than two observation days. When I began my internship, I quickly became very overwhelmed and thought I was just not going to get it. I would walk into the sterile core, stare at the endless rows of suture, and cry because I just knew I'd never memorize them all. Despite my doubts, I continued coming into work every day. I moved from graduate nurse to novice-level nurse, and somehow had acquired a little confidence in my abilities. Mind you, I was at the end of my internship. At this point, your preceptor allows you to fly solo within arm's length. When I learned the plan for the day, I suddenly became so anxious. My preceptor told me, "Okay! It is just you today! It's your show, run it! If you need me, I'll be here, but you're circulating on your own." My main preceptor was the lead orthopedic nurse, and since I was exposed to ortho every day, I developed a love for it and wanted to try my very best to learn all the things.

I was very high-strung and on edge the entire first case. My attending surgeon scrubs in and can see my obvious distress, and he says some encouraging words to me. I relaxed ever so slightly, the case started, and as I went about the room, the attending looks me dead in the face and says, "Oh my god, this is *horrible*! We need Krazy Glue. Go get Krazy Glue!" At that point, I never really questioned verbal orders since I assumed what they were asking for was just something I hadn't quite learned. I ran out of the room, saw my coworker and friend, and frantically asked them to point me to the Krazy Glue. He looked puzzled. He said, "Uh…I don't think that's a thing. Let's go back in there and find out what he's asking for." As we opened the door, everyone is laughing hysterically. My attending looked at me with a mischievous grin and apologized for being the one to initiate me into the OR. To this day, when I see him, he'll tell me to make sure there's Krazy Glue on his preference card.

The Surgeon Cell Phone Mishap

At the beginning of my career in the OR, I worked for a county hospital. Our facility was a teaching facility, so we had lots of residents and med students who would scrub in. On that particular day, my resident was on call but wanted to participate in the surgery. As luck would have it, his cell phone and pager went off during the case, and he conveniently had it attached to his waist. He's yelling at me to hurry up and reach under his gown from behind and grab the phone and pager. In a panic, I'm reaching into the back of his gown and around blindly in an attempt to retrieve the items. Unfortunately, in my hurry, I misjudged waist level and grabbed a handful of an unexpected surprise. I immediately released and backed off, but not before hearing my resident told me in a very high tone, "That's not it!" I have never apologized so quickly and repeatedly in a day. Both our faces were bright red, while we had a room full of roaring laughter. I never lived that incident down, and for the duration of my surgeon's residency, we could never fully look each other in the eye.

Trapped in a Box

We have a couple of rooms in our OR that are less than level, by any stretch of the imagination. So much so, when you release the brakes on the bed, it just drifts away to the other side of the room.

So I am assisting my hand surgeon one day, and I have my chair up too high to really get my feet planted because I am short and needed to be high enough to maintain my sterile field. Because the stool does not have brakes and I am at the patient's head, my chair just keeps rolling away, with me on it. So I keep having to grab the arm board and walk myself back into position with my hands about every three to five minutes. The surgeon just keeps giggling every time. Finally, he stops and says, "You look like a mime stuck in a box." I must admit, I did.

Why Isn't It Winking?

There was never a time in our OR that we didn't have someone learning a new skill. Medical students were revolving doors and walked in with specific tasks they personally wanted to attempt with assistance.

That particular day, we had a long case scheduled. My surgeon asked me to place a Foley catheter prior to preparing the patient for the procedure. My medical student was a very short, thin, yet determined man. My patient was a healthy woman with plenty of insulation, creating a bit of a challenge. My medical student was set on attempting the insertion of a Foley. He was determined. I agreed to assist him in his endeavor.

He begins preparing his tray and begins to talk very nervously. I can see he has suddenly become very anxious. With his sterile gloves straight in the air, he tells me he's going to try to expose the urethra. The poor guy is struggling but does not surrender. After multiple attempts he manages to get a suboptimal view of the urethra. He stops and says very loudly, "I thought it was supposed to wink. Why isn't it winking?"

For a few seconds, he's quiet then turns to me and confesses he's very unfamiliar with female anatomy of the nether areas. He says, "I do not have a girlfriend! I just don't know!" Despite his apprehensions, his effort and perseverance paid off. His forehead was sweaty, and his face looked relieved. He tells me, "Thank you for helping me. Girls are scary. I would never want to do this every day. It's a lot of work!" I tried with all my might not to laugh. I hope he overcame his fears. I was always curious as to what particular medical specialty he chose after graduating medical school. I'm assuming it wasn't OB or GYN.

Does This Condom Make Me Look Fat?

We had just got the kind of light handle covers that were flexible plastic and slid snugly over the attached handle. The vascular surgeon (who was not everyone's favorite to say the least) complains, "If condoms were this tight, no one would ever use them." Everyone looks at each other, I know what I wanted to say. Then anesthesia says it, "You know, George, most people think they are."

A Jar of Peanut Butter and a Dog

I was an instructor for a surgical technology program. I took a young student to her clinical site for the first time. We were assigned to a room preparing for a local vasectomy. The circulator was prepping the patient who was complimenting her attention to detail. The circulator told him how much she enjoys her job.

The patient responded that usually, to get this kind of attention, he needs a jar of peanut butter and his dog. I looked over at my student and said, "It actually gets worse than this sometimes…" I'll never forget the look on her face.

Open Your Eyes for Daddy

I was working with a CRNA who had two young daughters at home. He always talks to his patients in a soothing voice like he's talking to his daughters, but it works well in terms of putting his patient at ease. Anyway, we were waking up a patient after an ENT procedure, and he leans over and says calmly in the patient's ear, "Open your eyes for Daddy!"

We all stopped what we were doing and stared at him, he realized what he said and looked at us wide-eyed and red-faced, and we all burst out laughing. 😄

Perfect

A very experienced female circulator was training a new nurse in an ortho case. The patient was not asleep yet, and she lifted the sheet at the hip area to check the positioning. She said, "Perfect." The patient said, "Thanks."

Camel Toe

Twenty-three years ago, I was a young and naive nurse. I was assisting the surgeon and theater assistant, lifting the leg up for a tourniquet application, when I noticed a tattoo on the patient's left toe. I said to the staff (patient was anesthetized at this point), "That's a tattoo of a camel 🐫 on his toe" (big toe), which made several staff members laugh.

I asked them what was funny. They said, "That's a camel toe."

I said, "No, it's a camel on his toe."

Then someone had to explain what it meant. Obviously, I lived under a rock and didn't know the meaning. Staff told me to go home and research it lol. 😄

I went home and asked my husband. He laughed for ten minutes, until I was visibly irritated with him, then he explained. Lol 😄 , hmmmm no wonder they all laughed.

Step Stool Fail

I was scrubbed with a neurosurgeon. We both were standing on a step stool. He stepped off his and bumped me. I then fell off my step stool and could not get my balance. I kept walking backward until I hit the trash can and fell. There were also two trays by the trash can that fell on my head. It was hilarious. The trays did not hurt my head. I could not quit laughing.

After everyone saw I was okay, they joined in on the laughter!

Back Scratcher

Brand-new OR nurse working in ortho suite, super eager to do well and please. Surgeon says to the scrub tech, "I need a back scratcher."

Yup, nurse proceeds to carefully scratch surgeon's back. Lesson 1, make sure they are talking to you! lmao

Not All Curettes Are Created the Same

Gyn nurse circulating my ortho case. I asked for curettes; she brought me the gyn curettes. Even the ortho surgeon got a good laugh out of that.

Bulldog

I was scrubbing a huge ortho case. Just started as a traveler (usually do cardiac). Surgeon asks me for a "bulldog." I start looking around for those vascular bulldogs. I finally asked him why in the heck does he need those little vascular bulldog clamps! Never knew those giant wire drivers were called bulldogs. Now when my favorite cardiac surgeon asks for a bulldog. I make sure I have the giant wire driver just for him!

Time Out

Working a general case, and the surgeon had his new graduate finally gown and glove, he was so excited you could see him smile through his mask. He's very smart and quite witty. It's time to close up the wound, and the tech was getting more sutures ready. The surgeon asked the new graduate a question while he was closing up, and since the graduate didn't know the answer, he stepped back, crossed his arms in his pits.

We said, "You contaminated yourself." He apologized and then he put himself in time out facing the wall and scolding himself. Now the surgeon and everyone is laughing, and the surgeon's laugh is not a cute laugh; it's one of those ugly laughs. And now we are all laughing at the surgeon instead of the grad. When the case was over, and we were cleaning up, the new grad was still standing in his corner lol.

Three Holes

Doing a gyn case, and the new graduate, very green and inexperienced (with the ladies), was doing the prep and asked why there are three holes. Even the anesthesia stopped breathing lol. Never a dull moment in the operating room.

Street Legal

Once had an NFL player in for Achilles repair. As we pushed the propofol, he lifts his head and says, "Woo-wee, that shit ain't street legal," and he's out. 😴😴😴

Big Guy

One time while working with a pretty religious surgeon, he walks in and looks at the patient on the table, and he says, "Wow, you're a big guy!" The patient (right before intubation) chimes in, "I have a big dick too." 😳 🙈

Clitoris

Sometimes, the funniest things are misspoken words. Orderly watching anesthesia intubating the patient asked, "Do you ever hit the clitoris when you do that?" Anesthesia, without missing a beat, "Only if the patient is really short."

Everyone laughs hysterically. Orderly still stands there, not understanding what we are laughing about, which made it even funnier.

Screw Loose

Working at a new facility, doing a GYN case. The doc was sitting down, and I'm standing next to him. I glanced down and noticed he was about to lose the screw on his glasses. So I innocently say "Doctor, you have a screw loose." He stopped what he was doing, looked at me, and said, "No one has ever said that to my face before." Thankfully he laughed.

*****

I was working with a surgeon who is known to have a good personality and I had a pretty good rapport with. We were doing a hand case, so we were both seated.

His stool kept squeaking and sinking lower and lower. I looked at him, not even thinking, I said, "I think you have a screw loose, doctor." He cocked his head and said to me, with a straight face, "That's a little personal, but duh." Everyone laughed.

Oral or Vaginal

Doing a vaginal hysterectomy under spinal (that anesthesia provider preferred spinals whenever possible). The patient was unusually chatty, but we weren't really paying attention. She was babbling something about hormone therapy when she loudly said, "Dr. R., when you give it to your women, do you prefer orally or vaginally?"

I thought the surgeon was going to fall off his seat laughing.

No Bitches for an Ace

After a knee scope on an eighteen-year-old boy, he woke up in the OR and asked me what kind of bandage he had on. I told him it was an Ace bandage.

He deadass sat up and looked at me and said, "Man. Ace wraps won't get me no bitches." And then lay back down. The CRNA was mortified, and I died laughing.

Faster

I was new to the OR. My scrub tech said, "I need a 5-0 fast." I proceeded to open a 5-0 chromic quickly. She said "No, I need a 5-0 fast."

So I open the 5-0 chromic even faster!

Nope, I need a 5-0 plain gut fast-absorbing suture.

She just stood there with a completely clueless look on her face. She had no idca what fast-absorbing suture was. The doc looked up at her, looked back at me, and asked, "Is she rebooting?"

Rougher Than My Husband

Moving a patient (little old lady) over to the OR bed, and she made it about halfway before giving up. Her shoulders made it, but her bottom half was still on the stretcher. The surgeon lifted her by the hips to bring her over the rest of the way, and her eyes popped open and she goes, "You're rougher than my husband!"

"Wait, cadaver bone? [long pause] I hope I don't get haunted"

Legos or Ninja Turtles

Last night, while working the night shift, we had a case come in with free air in the abdomen. Naturally, we took him to the OR to do an exploratory laparotomy. The doctor started running the bowel to check for a perforation and filled an entire-liter suction container in less than fifteen minutes from the OG tube. On his way down the right colon, he found three very hard objects that appeared to be squarish in shape.

The perforation was just below the last one, obviously caused by the object. The discussion started with me and the medical student guessing what was inside. My guess was big Legos; his guess was action figures (Ninja Turtle action figures to be exact). At this point, I pointed out the obvious, that there are four Ninja Turtles and only three foreign objects. "Maybe he passed the other one," he suggested.

We were both incorrect, of course. I laid out an area on my back table for the doctor to dissect the section of bowel to find out what it was. As he was pulling it out and trying to spread the object out, it sounded crinkly like paper. Soon he announced that it was an exam glove, a used exam glove, as the fingers were inside out. All three objects were gloves.

After returning to the field and continuing his examination of the small intestine and the stomach, he was able to feel more objects in the stomach. Another doctor came in and they gastroscopically removed five more from the stomach.

As we started to close up, I suggested that maybe we should send him home with a box of gloves to go—"Road snacks," I said. This landed like a fart in church. So I said, "Too soon?" Again, a fart in church, literally; I work in a very religious hospital. More often than not, I find myself way more hilarious than anyone else does.

Shirtless Surgeon

I was fresh off orientation and working a call shift. We had been having issues with getting scrubs at our hospital, and everyone was pretty fed up with it. I was setting up an emergency hysterectomy and not really listening to anesthesia or the nurse complaining about the scrub situation until everything went very quiet, and then a very loud snort, followed by laughter. I turned around to see my quite rotund older doctor standing just inside the door with nothing on but scrub pants, suspenders, and crocs. "No shirts my size," he said.

Mussels

One of our anesthesiologists' favorite stories to tell is the day he decided to eat smoked mussels for lunch and then went into a really long case. The mussels must have been bad because he was sweating bullets trying to hold it together and ended up leaving the OR shuffling both legs in a trash bag because he couldn't keep it together, if you catch my drift.

Jokes

This just happened several weeks ago. (Not sure if you can use it in your book, but it made my day). A very large patient. After I got her settled on the OR table, she informed me that she was so nervous she needed to tell me a joke because laughing calmed her down (we were waiting on anesthesia for some reason).

"Actually," she said, "this really happened to me the other day. I dropped something on my bathroom floor and knelt down to pick it up. As soon as I was on the floor, I had the most intense chest pain! I thought, 'Oh boy, this is it! The angels are here to take me away.' I was convinced I was having a heart attack till I realized I was just kneeling on my nipple!" One of the funniest stories a patient has ever told me.

Stupid or Just Don't Care

Years ago, I worked with a surgeon who could be a curmudgeon. One day, at the end of a case, he told the circulator and scrub in his room, "Are you guys stupid, or do you just not care?" Thirty minutes later, when he entered the room to start his next case, there they were, each with a piece of tape on their OR hats with "Stupid" on one and "Don't Care" on the other. He left them alone after that.

A Little Prick

The same curmudgeon surgeon was removing a Bartholin cyst under local with sedation. I handed him the syringe with local, and he really said, standing between the patient's legs (lithotomy) "Ma'am, you're going to feel a little prick." We never let him live that down. It came up at the most inopportune times.

Propofol Always Wins

So not the only patient, but my favorite patients are the ones who ask to know when we push the "sleepy juice" because, and I quote, "I'm going to fight it!" Anesthesia looks up when the patient falls asleep. "Propofol always wins."

I Stole Her Pen

I had an emergency surgery in the hospital where I work, and OR where I work. In fact, my preceptor was my RN for my case. Apparently, I am quite funny under anesthesia, quite the rolling comedy show.

I don't remember, but apparently, the PACU RN (also one of my friends) said my preceptor had just dropped me off and was giving a report when she lost her pen, she was looking everywhere for it.

I loudly whisper, like a drunk girl who thinks she is whispering, "Don't tell her. I stole her pen." Then giggled really loud.

You Don't Know What I Drive

After midnight one night while working with a surgeon who is very well known to be very meticulous and slow. While suturing a bowel anastomosis, the surgeon cut the suture out to start over, after taking over two hours to suture it to begin with. (Doesn't use the stapler because the suture holds better, according to him.) So I ask the circulator to get me twenty more 5-0 prolene sutures.

He goes another two hours and almost has it finished again, asks for the scissors, and cuts it all back out again. The air is so tense in the room now, between anesthesia's frustration with him telling the CRNA four hours ago that we would be done in about an hour, and me, the scrub tech, shooting daggers out of my eyes. So I ask the circulator once again for another twenty more 5-0 prolene sutures.

Two hours goes by, and he is almost finished again. He asks for the scissors. As I hold them in my hand, I make eye contact with him and hold on to the scissors, I proceed to tell him, "If you cut all that suture out again, I am going to slash your tires." Anesthesia slowly sinks down to the other side of the drape, trying not to lose it.

The doctor looks at me with a straight face and says, "You don't know what I drive." OMG.

Side note: He did not cut the suture out again, and he drives a white Toyota 4Runner. *Hehehe!* Oh yes, I do!

Not Fucking Pregnant

Here, I am forty-eight years old, new to this hospital, and waiting for my dosimetry badge to come in. Finally, one day my radiology tech says, "Hey, your dosimetry badges are in the lounge." I'm assuming that she is talking to both myself and the other tech that was standing with me. My break time comes, and I go to the lounge only to see that I have been ordered two badges.

So I put one in the bag and write a note stating that there must be a mistake and I was ordered two instead of one. The next time they come, again two badges. I put one in the bag with the same note. This happens for about eighteen months.

I go to pick up my badge(s) in the lounge, my back turned to everyone, not realizing how quiet it is and how loud I am, I say, "I'm not fucking pregnant, I am just fat." The lounge erupts in laughter. Oops, guess I'll just wait here for HR.

My Wife Drives a Subaru

There's an orthopedic surgeon that I work(ed) with quite a lot, and he does not really have a very joking personality. On a call night, he had come in to repair a traumatic injury to a shoulder.

My nurse that evening, also a man, and anesthesia, also a man, so I was the only female in the room. The doctor had put in a wire and had decided that he would keep it in, so he asked me for a pair of dykes.

I looked at my back table and stated, "No Subaru drivers here."

Surgeon said, "My wife drives a Subaru!" as he has completely stopped operating to make eye contact with me.

"Oh!" I said sheepishly. Would have been fantastic if that was where it ended, but nooo, I had to keep going.

> Circulator: My wife also drives a Subaru!
> Me: Oh, do they know each other?
> Everyone: (Crickets)

Side note: I am not against lesbians. I am bisexual myself. I was just trying to be funny. No longer one of his regular scrub techs after that. Some people just can't take a joke.

I'm Just Going to Tell People You Got Me Wet

Standing at the scrub sink, scrubbing with one of my friends, first thing in the morning, chatting away, oblivious to one of my favorite general surgeons sneaking up behind us. Previously I had been on a medical mission with said surgeon, so we had some running jokes and some incidents to get even for. For instance, I had filled his sterile gloves with sterile lube and gloved him with them.

So when he saw me not paying attention at the scrub sink, he saw an opportunity and he seized it. Now I weigh about 120 pounds, and I'm 5'2" tall. He ran up, scooped me up in his arms, and dumped me into the running sink.

As he walked away cackling his evil laugh, I just yelled down the hall, "I'm telling everyone you got me wet."

He stopped laughing, shook his head, and said, "Damn it! I did not see that backfiring."

I got the last laugh, and so did my friend. Never mess with an old scrub.

Am I Obese?

I had an anesthesiologist standing over a patient getting ready to put her to sleep, and he started talking about why obese patients are risky. The patient looked up at him and asked if she was obese. He said, "Yes!" and the lights went out. OMG.

Sit, Stay

I had taken my patient to PACU. When I finished the report, he wakes up, flips over on all fours, and starts barking and growling.

Two Front Teeth

Surgeon: Tell [circulator] to call the ICU and ask about the next patient's CT."

Circulator on the phone with ICU: "I have no idea why, but the doctor wants to know about the patient's *two front teeth*."

Bam

During the IMA (internal mammary artery) takedown, I asked my circulator, "Can I have a malleable?"

Circulator said, "Sure" (leaves…then returns …) and ☼ *bam* on my back table… "Well…you asked for a mallet!" 😂😂😂

Typical

Keeping the pump primed till last minute. Pumper sending me the blood to suck to the cell saver. *Oops!* Line slipped—had to save it. Elbow knocked blood over the side onto the perfusionist's head.

He said, "That's typical of how this case has gone."

Cephalad

Working at an OPSC, like, ten years ago. Patient is eightyish years old, sedated in MAC. Small basal cell removal. Surgeon is old, grumpy, crotchety. Screams at the circulator "White suture is lateral, black suture is cephalad!" She asks him to repeat, so he angrily slams his instruments down and repeats.

Patient responds, "Cephalllaaaddd!" in this long, croaky voice. Old, crabby pants gets wide-eyed and backs away laughing.

I Told You So

I was working with a neurosurgeon, and I had just given her the implant. Her glasses were halfway down her nose, so I said, "Hey, doc. Your glasses are about to fall off."

She looks at me and says, "No, they're not! Look!"

She starts dancing around and her glasses fell right off her face and onto the wound.

We all just stopped and stared for a bit, had a laugh, some "I told you so," and did our best to fix the sterility issue. 😂😂😂 We still talk about it to this day.

Extended Warranty

During a case in which we sent a frozen specimen to pathology. While waiting for the pathologist to call back, the phone rings in the OR, and the nurse immediately puts it on speaker. "We're calling you about your car's extended warranty." I lost it. Surgeon didn't find it as funny.

Open Your Eye

I was scrubbed in a case that I normally circulate, and when it was over our foreign anesthesiologist was waking the patient, telling them "Open your eye" over and over. I couldn't resist. I turned around and said, "Just one eye, doctor?" The room burst out laughing, so every case after that, when he was waking the patient up, he would say it once, then look around to see if I was in the room, then he would start saying eyes.

Chicks Dig Slings

One of my favs—fixed a shoulder on a college athlete, and the first thing he said when he woke up was "Chicks dig slings."

But *No One* Died

Trauma and endovascular thoracic aneurysm case in the trauma room. The patient is under the hybrid C-arm table, and the table isn't able to move the C-arm head away from the patient's chest. The patient goes into a shockable rhythm. The patient does not have AED pads placed. The surgeon screams, "You are killing the patient!" This was directed at anesthesia. The rad tech is trying to troubleshoot the table and C-arm.

A trauma nurse brings in defib paddles, and a trauma scrub assembles them and brings them to me, the CV scrub. I'm like, "No, thank you. The chest isn't open. There's no way we are using those without a saw first. Take those back to your table. I'm not taking them." Chaos is the only way to describe what was happening in the room.

It was pretty funny since no one died. The patient did go back to a stable rhythm, but it was interesting to say the least. I now make sure every patient has AED pads on in that room whenever I'm in there supporting trauma.

The doc finished up the case and afterward looked at us and said, "Well, that's giving a new meaning to, but did you die?" Yes. Yes, I did, but the patient lived. I guess you just must have some comedy to relieve the stress of the situation.

One Crock out the Door

I was circulating a shoulder scope, and this one slightly portly anesthesia doctor always walks swiftly with no purpose, but in a scope room that is dangerous.

He swiftly walked into the puddle of water that is steadily getting bigger, slips, his feet literally go up in the air, one crock flying through the air and landing outside the door as it was closing. The suction goes up in the air, and he looked like a turtle on its back waving his arms and squirming, trying to get up.

We all stopped to make sure he was okay. The minute he left the room, everyone was hysterical. I peed a little. Okay, maybe a lot.

Santa HoHo

Favorite OR story of mine. We have a toddler having a T&A. Now we're used to comfort items for kids and encourage them for surgery, like a binkie, stuffed animal, blanket... Well, this kid's is a two-foot wooden statue of Santa Claus. She calls him Santa HoHo.

As we're getting ready to take her back to the OR, the CRNA says that Santa HoHo should help the parents find the popsicles for the patient. She gets a little teary, and I say, "Oh no. Santa HoHo made it this far, Santa HoHo is getting the full experience." The kid has the biggest smile on her face while we go back to the OR and doesn't fuss while she goes to sleep.

The scrub then secured Santa HoHo to the crib with Coban so that when she wakes up, he'll be there.

The best part is, it's the middle of March. So this munchkin has had Santa HoHo with her for at least three months.

A Story You Will Never Hear in Chicago

"Well…I was makin' moonshine, and my still blew up, and my foot caught on fire. And my mule ranned away. And I lost my cell phone. So I had to walk through the woods to get home."

How Did He Not Hit the Microscope?

Twilight sedation for cataract surgery. This guy is about three minutes into an eight-minute case. He has been silent and still since the Versed went in. Suddenly, the man sits up, grabs the drape and rips it off his face. The eye speculum goes flying! He looks around and starts to lie back down as the CRNA and circulator rush to the table, and the surgeon starts cussing and yelling.

The patient bonks his head on the microscope on the way back to supine; how he missed it on the way up I still don't know. Shockingly, his only self-inflicted injury was a subconjunctival hemorrhage from the speculum. He also got general anesthesia for his second eye procedure.

Is This Normal?

The first cataract surgery I saw as a tech, the patient jerked, and I was like, "Ohhh crap." My butthole puckered. 💀😬 The surgeon was not a happy camper! I remember being very surprised, and everyone just kept going on like normal.

Top or Bottom

I was working with an ortho surgeon that was a bit difficult at times. I didn't work with him very often; ortho wasn't my favorite. This day I got stuck in his room. We were doing an open shoulder repair. I was the tech. I didn't know where he wanted me to stand to be of most help. As we were draping, I said, "Do you want me on the top or the bottom?"

Just as the last words were out of my mouth, I turned to him and waited. He didn't disappoint… because he gave me a very odd, puzzled look and said, "Depends on what we are talking about?" Everyone in the room laughed.

I think he was a little worried how I'd taken it, but I probably laughed the loudest. It was one of the better days in this surgeon's room.

Poop Emoji

I am an OR nurse and had my gallbladder out two weeks ago. My surgeon also happens to be a really funny guy. I told him to make sure and take pics so I could see my gallbladder too… Well, he took plenty. In fact, he got this little poop emoji and set it next to my gallbladder after the case and they said he worked so hard to get it lined up for the pic.

After surgery, the entire crew in my room had me convinced that the poop emoji was *in* my gallbladder!

I said, "Well, no wonder it didn't work!" 💩

It was a good three hours until I was thinking straight enough to realize they were kidding!

Crickets

Belgian fellow was in the room during a neuro case. The incredibly volatile chairman came through the room to see how things were going, since we were operating on a VIP.

> Anesthesia: Hello, William.
> Surgeon: Hello, Bill.
> Nurse: Hey, Willie.
> Belgian Fellow (in rich Belgian accent): Doctor, I hear them call you Bill, Will, Billy, and William. But tell me, where do they get Dick from?

You could have heard a pin drop as Billy stopped and locked the door. (Cue song reference: Kenny Rogers) LOL

Mom and Toner

I watched an eighteen-year-old sit up, spit out his LMA, and make a statement about his mom and toner.

Med Student Fail

A med student came to watch a case. We asked if he wanted to scrub in. He was ready and said he knew how. He asked where the eye protection was kept. We had the masks with the plastic face shield extension. There is quite a bit of distortion and reflection when you wear the cone of safety, so we used to just flip it over and wear it as a shield and sweatband. No fogging. No distortion.

She told the med student to flip it over and put it on over his eyes. He followed directions great. He came stumbling in with the mask completely over both eyes, and the shield covering his nose and mouth. The scrub busted up, and then the whole room turned to watch as he fumbled his way to a wall.

You Need a Step for That

I got thrown into a case with two services and a scrub that didn't know either service very well. I was missing so much stuff for both surgeons. Started running my nurse for supplies. I had a good portion of what I needed but of course I missed one item, and the nurse was out getting the last list of things I had asked for.

The doctor was frustrated by now as they had nothing he needed and now it looked like I was going to hose him as well. He walked over to the wall and asked, "Is this where Dr. Bush beats his head on the wall?"

I said, "You're too short to reach up there, and we don't have a step up without the nurse."

Catch That Cat!

We had just finished a hernia surgery on a young female. I was cleaning up my back table and I hear her groaning. Anesthesia asked for me to stand bedside since the patient was waking up. As I was standing next to her…she sits straight up on the OR bed and asks me, "did you see that cat?" I said no sorry. She says, "catch that cat, she just shit in my mouth and ran off." Then lays down like nothing happened. Hahaha!

How Many Anesthesiologists Does It Take to Intubate a Patient?

X-ray here! I also helped with prepping the patient so mine might be a little different. We had just moved the patient to the table, and anesthesia just put them under. The first (this is key) anesthesiologist was having difficulty intubating the patient, so another one was called in to assist and bring in the video-guided machine (glidescope).

Three more anesthesiologists wind up coming in, so there are now five all together, and the surgeon is getting mad. I'm sitting on my C-arm and joked with the surgeon and circulator to help alleviate the tension. Four of the five anesthesiologists are now on their phones googling something, and the surgeon gets mad (how could he not?). And one of the anesthesiologists finally gets the patient intubated.

So I asked the surgeon, "How many anesthesiologists does it take to intubate a patient?"

He glared at me, "How many?"

"One, the other four are too busy on their phones."

He actually laughed, and so did the anesthesiologists, we had a great crew.

You Can Put My Loops On Now

Training a new peri-op nurse. Neurosurgeon says, "Okay, you can put my loops on now." Yup, she did—*on her head!* He had to walk away from the field, laughing so hard. I almost wet myself. She became a good OR nurse.

AFLAC

I was doing a case with two general surgeons. One of them coughed and farted, very loudly at the same time. The fart echoed.

Anesthesia popped his head over the drape. "What was that?" He asked. The guilty doc said "AFLAC!"

We all laughed till we cried and then carried on, with more intermittent spurts of laughter.

A Rifle?

I was circulating a laparoscopic GYN case, and they asked for a Vicryl suture. Didn't have that particular one in the room. I told the scrub tech I was going to run and get her that Vicryl. The surgeon stopped what she was doing, looked over, and said, "You're going to get a rifle?" 😂😂😂 Things we think we hear versus what was said. LOL

Amazon

Had a man tell me, "Amazon is only getting one star!" This was on the way to recovery after we had removed a dildo from his butt!

The Scrub Room

I used to work with an ENT who was a great surgeon and a good friend. We teased each other a lot and had a great time during his cases. He was doing a nose/sinus case, and I was trying to stand in the most convenient place. I said "Where should I stand to be the most help to you?" His reply? "In the scrub room!" The rest of staff was a bit shocked, but we both thought it was funny!

Still Here

Nurses as patients… My former boss had surgery and was extremely nervous. As we brought her to PACU, she sat bolt upright and started taking her pulse. I said, "All is well! What are you doing?"

"Making sure I'm still alive."

She did this off and on for about five minutes, letting us all know she was still here. 😄

Rap Music in the OR

If you don't already know, we do most of the time, listen to music during an operation. Depending on the surgeon's preference, normally.

We had a neurosurgeon who really liked rap. Not just any rap—it had to be gangster rap. The more uses of the word *fuck* and the *N*-word the better.

After about two hours of this one day, my nurse looked at him and said, "We have to change this music."

He looked at her and asked, "Does the F-word offend you?"

She looked him square in the eye and said, "*No*, but if we don't change this soon, I am going to rob a fucking liquor store on my way home."

I literally blew snot all over the inside of my mask. We all just erupted in laughter.

From that day on, she was allowed to choose the music when we worked with him, so old ass country music it was. Still not sure which was worse.

I'm My Own SCDs

I had neck surgery and when I finally began to realize I was in PACU, my nurse said, "Gee, you must have run a marathon by now." I asked what he meant.

He said, "The minute you hit PACU, you started moving your legs like you were running."

Ohhh…I was worried about getting blood clots (subconsciously), and this was me under drugs trying to prevent them.

So Much for Discreet

New circulator here. Was on orientation when the surgeon dropped a ring forceps on the floor. When I bent down to pick it up my front closure bra unhooked, and being a bit busty, my boob literally popped out of my scrub top. Hoping I could discreetly walk into our attached substerile room and hook her back up and go back to work. I looked up, and my male scrub tech and anesthesia were both looking at me with what I can only assume was wide open mouths by the way their eyes looked.

I now always wear an undershirt.

Yeah, but What Does the Inside Look Like?

I am a surgical tech, that got called in to do a case at 2:00 a.m. one night. Surgeon comes into the room, looks at me, and says, "You are going to love this one." He refused to explain further. Patient comes wheeling into the room with a knife in his gut, wrapped in paper towels and tin foil. He looked at us and asked if we were going to save his life.

We had to ask the patient why there was a knife sticking out of his midsection, like, was he attacked or fell on it, or what? Nothing prepares you for some of the answers.

He said, he wanted to see what looked like inside! Turns out, the knife was a good twelve inches long, crammed to the hilt inside this guy. Somehow or another, he missed every single organ in his entire body. Did not even nick the bowel!

Bobby Pin

The kiddo was maybe seven years old, and we'd have a full day of pedi urology cases already scheduled. The resident got a page during turnover, came back to the room and warned us that there may be a change in the schedule.

Apparently, in the ED, the kid was open and honest about it all. He had wanted to see if his pee could actually push something solid out of his body. So he stuck a bobby pin up his urethra and somehow managed to get it stuck.

Resident was almost able to get it out in the ED, but ended up needing to take them back to the OR for a quick cysto, grabbed the bobby pin, did a quick look around, no other damage, and sent the kid home just without the bobby pin.

Sharpened Big Black Dildo

Wife and husband came into the ED, apparently looking sheepish and a little awkward (per the ACS resident). Resident was told that the couple was having some fun in the shower and the husband "slipped and fell" onto the dildo.

They couldn't get it out at home, and the hubby started to not feel great, so they came in. Took an X-ray, and it was immediately obvious that the dildo had perforated the bowel.

When the resident told them that he would need surgery as he had a hole in his bowel, the wife said something along the lines of, "Oh, maybe we should not have sharpened it after all."

The surgery was pretty straightforward. Easy to repair tear, hadn't hit anything else. The dildo was easy to find as well, considering it was rather large, black, and indeed sharpened. I'm sure pathology had a laugh at that one. Can't remember if the couple asked for it back or not.

Side note: How do you sharpen a dildo? Asking for a friend.

Bad Drugs and a Fat Wad of Cash

I did a lady who was tweaking on a few drugs and was an exotic dancer, and where is the best place to put a fat bankroll of money from work? Well, she became rather uncomfortable with this bankroll in her vagina, and she could not get it out. So instead of using the obvious choice of her fingers and kegels to get the bankroll out, she jumped to the next best thing. Can you guess?

Needle-nose pliers! So she took a pair of needle-nose pliers up her vagina to get this bankroll out. She did not succeed in her endeavor multiple times and tore up her vaginal walls.

We took her in emergent, she was bleeding really bad after we found out the drugs she was tweaking on and took the bankroll out. This thing was about two to three inches tight-rolled worth of assorted bills covered in blood. Everyone asked what to do with the money, I said, "Put it in a bio bag and let her take it home and wash it. She's more than earned it."

We repaired her vaginal walls where she tore them and sent the money with her to PACU.

The Straw That Broke the Camel's Back

Another was a fungating tumor in the elbow from SCC from repeated IV drug use and infection. This thing was more than just fungating, this elbow was rotten. You could see the olecranon and the head of the radius clear as day and dead and rotting out of this elbow.

You wonder at what point was the straw that broke the camel's back? Was it the black tissue surrounding the dead bone, or the atrocious smell? Was it the dead bone? Not entirely sure, but the doctor removed the nastiness of that elbow, put in an antibiotic spacer with what was left of viable tissue. Later he came in for an elbow replacement. Amazingly he still has feeling in his hand and forearm.

Happy

You can have this one if you want it. Years ago, when I was still a baby scrub tech, we had a male patient for an inguinal hernia repair (open procedure). The nurse pulled the sheet back to prep him, and on the tip of his penis was one of those sticker tattoo Band-Aid things, and it was a bright-yellow smiley face. Happy for all the world to see.

Bat Thighs

When I had my hysterectomy I wanted to tape a bat 🦇 on the inside of my thigh, but I knew the nurse who was my circulator and thought she'd panic and beat me with a boom or something. 🦇

Shoe Covers for Admin

While escorting someone from admin around the OR to look for pieces of equipment that she had to locate, someone at the nurse's desk looked up and said, "You are an asshole." I was so confused that after I finished with the girl and escorted her out, I went back to the nurse's desk to ask what prompted this odd but not off-base comment.

She then showed me a picture on her phone of me walking away with the admin person. Turns out she had been wearing a shoe cover on her head the whole time, and I never noticed. The charge nurse just assumed, because it was me that I knew and chose not to tell her, since this seemed to track with my usual behavior.

Extended Warranty

Found this on a patient. It was a Post-it note, in the belly button, "We have been trying to reach you about your extended car warranty."

Smoke Break

I came into the room to give a break at the end of a hand or arm case. We rolled the patient to get them back onto the stretcher and a whole pack of cigarettes fell out of their gown.

Clothes On

Came up to the hospital in street clothes for education stuff. Surgeon saw me from across the waiting room and screamed, "Girl, I almost didn't recognize you with clothes on!" I almost died.

This happened to me too! A CRNA I worked with was quite the funny guy and saw me at the checkout line at the grocery store. We were about three checkouts apart, and it was rush hour and busy. He yelled the same thing toward me. Everyone stopped, turned to look at my red face, then most of them laughed. A few of the older members of my church that were in line didn't seem to think it was quite that funny. I had to explain later why it was considered funny to me and my family!

Blow on It

We were doing a GYN robot case, and in the room was a nurse who wasn't too sharp. Flighty, most may say.

The nurse is plugging everything in that I threw off the field, and she looks at the PK cord suspiciously after trying to plug it in multiple times and failing. She's looking a little flustered, so I say in the most sincere tone that I can muster, "Listen, sometimes it gets shit in the opening. Blow on it, then try."

Now through her mask, we hear her go *phheewww* and inadvertently, she happens to turn the cord over, so when she goes to plug it in, it works. I swear on my eyes, she seriously thought she did it by blowing on it. That was ten years ago, and we still laugh about it.

Pants on the Ground

After a long lap chole, my really slow general surgeon stepped away from the field to break scrub. He looked down and saw my pants around my ankles. He looked up at my face and said, "Are those your pants?"

I looked at him and without changing my face at all, I responded with, "No, I had Mary put these around my feet when we got bored an hour in."

From that day on, he started timing himself for every lap chole.

Hot Mama

When I was new to the hospital, I was working with an orthopedic surgeon. At one point during a shoulder scope, he asked, "Can I get a hot mama?"

I was left speechless. I did not know if he was being flirty, messing with me, or joking with the room at my expense. After a couple of minutes, he asked if I got his hot mama yet. I responded, "Yeah, I'm right here."

Turns out he calls the ArthroCare wand used to coagulate bleeders while doing scope procedures "Hot Mama." Guess who felt like a complete idiot and did not live it down for over a year, until I did something even dumber that overshadowed it. (i.e., the story about the Subaru and a pair of dykes)

But Wait, There's More

So it's the middle of the night, and I get a call to the emergency room to do a traction pin. I get it set up, while the doc is injecting some local into the patient's thigh muscle.

As he starts to drill into the patient's muscles, he begins to really scream. Me, not the best at dealing with people, pop off with "But wait, there's more."

The doc looks up at me and says, "This is why you work with patients who are asleep."

Richard

Three o'clock in the morning, we get the call that we have a full trauma coming in from about thirty minutes away and that it's a gunshot wound. Of course, no one says the area of the body, so we normally assume it is a head wound and probably self-inflicted, given the time and that the bars closed over an hour ago.

We set up the trauma room for a crani and wait. My charge nurse goes to the emergency department to await our trauma. Fifteen minutes later, she calls me and says, "It's going to be an open belly."

I rush to get the right trauma carts and get the horseshoe off the bed. I am just scrubbed in when they roll into the room with the patient, and he is belligerent, screaming, "I need to call my wife! I have to tell her that I love her!"

Now this patient was shot in the belly, by the police when they responded to a domestic disturbance where the husband was waving around a gun *at his wife*. My CRNA—let's call him David—keeps telling him, no, he can't make a phone call from the operating room.

This guy gets really mad and yells at David, "*What's your name?*"

Without missing a beat, he says "Richard." Then he starts pushing propofol. I thought I was going to pee. I was laughing so hard.

After the patient is asleep, I look up at him and I say, "Richard?"

With all the seriousness in the world, he says "I don't want him to come back and murder me."

CHAPTER 5

KARMA

Knocked the Fuck Out

I was on call and was called in to go relieve another scrub who was in the process of setting up for an I&D/Wash-Out, so that he could go set up and do the urgent vascular case that just posted since he was on the vascular team. He tells me the case is a simple wash-out, and he has the back table all set up and ready and that it should be easy-peasy.

When the surgeon comes into the OR, it turns out to be the vascular surgeon whom I had never worked with since I was not on the vascular team and typically didn't do vascular cases. The surgeon has his "new" resident with him, and once he sees he is not working with his "team," he takes one look at my back table and immediately starts yelling that anytime I'm scrubbing his case, I should open all his vascular pans, along with other supplies he starts demanding we have in the room and opened.

He turns to the circulator and starts yelling out all the supplies he wants opened up, and she is scurrying around to get the items plus tie him up and do the time-out so that we can get started. He, of course, is growing more impatient by the minute and is just yelling and fussing about everything. He and the resident start opening the incision and washing it out, all while the circulator is running around gathering more suture, vessel loops, vascular pans part 1 and part 2, and I am setting all this up while counting instruments and trying to keep him happy. He is yelling over the top of our counts and has his resident so nervous, that his hands are shaking, and several times he almost drops his forceps off the field.

I'm finally counted and set up, and really trying to help the nervous resident when the surgeon yells at the top of his lungs that the light handle got contaminated by his resident's scrub hat and wants another light handle. The circulator opens another light handle and grabs the OR light to remove the contaminated light handle, and then pushes the light back over to where I can put the new light handle cover on. The surgeon is complaining he doesn't have enough light and we are taking too long, so the nervous resident grabs the light handle and jerks it away from us to try to put the light back on the field. However, he is overzealous, and slams the OR light into the vascular surgeon's head and dang near knocked him out.

The surgeon steps back about four feet from the OR table, turns his back to the field, leans over to keep from passing out, and is cussing under his breath.

Good thing we wear masks, because I was laughing inside my mask, as was the circulating nurse. The resident just froze and didn't know what to do. After several minutes, the surgeon turned around and walked back over to the OR table, asked for a needle driver and suture to start closing, because it was just a simple wash-out, and never said another word. For a moment, I kinda just wanted to hug that resident.

After running the poor circulator to death and having us open all those pans/supplies and doing counts while he is yelling at us, all I can say is *karma* 😊.

Racist Doc Gets What He Deserves

One really arrogant new ortho doc was complaining about the size of the patient. Her ethnic background 👀, her financial status, blah, blah… On and on… She had fallen and broken her ankle badly. And it was hugely swollen, with the added problem of edema.

Sooo he's following my favorite doc, who was there to assist 😬.

"This woman should have gone to the tribal clinic."

"Can you believe she has kids? Kids! Well, some black guy was with her."

"She has Medicaid of course."

Now there's me, who's fluffy and has mixed kids, and my bestie, who is Native, standing there listening to this *I-D-I-O-T*, and the other surgeon is shaking his head at me right when he says, "OMG, how is it possible…to get pregnant…"

I say quietly, "Maybe you gotta actually have a dick."

Anesthesia snatches the drape clips, and the drape moves up so he could hide.

"Who…in the fuck would want…to get someone like this pregnant?"

My neck was about to roll! Well, I'm fat, and I've got plenty of children. I've never had a problem…ever…in life. You must be single…and definitely lacking."

My doc says, "You asked for that."

The arrogant ortho says, "What?"

They Don't Like Us Putting the Live Ones in a Bag

Okay, so basically everyone who works in the medical field has a sense of humor that could be considered a little bit off-putting. But add night/graveyard shift on top of that off-putting sense of humor, and you get just absolutely wrong. Taking this into consideration, I tell you the next installment of "I Am an Asshole."

Working night shift—graveyard shift it used to be called—takes a special kind of person. I am this person, but there are nights that test my resilience. This is the story of such a night. Please remember when you read this that we use a morbid sense of humor to hide uncomfortable feelings sometimes.

I arrived to work one evening to find that there was an organ procurement happening. This was not abnormal. It was a very busy night, and the procurement team did not need our staff to help, so we went about our other duties and surgeries.

When the team was finished, they left the body in the room, as the eye procurement team would be following them, but they were still a couple hours from arriving. This was not conveyed to the cleaning staff, who do not participate in surgery and are thus not numb to seeing someone deceased, alone in an OR that they were now alone *with.* This resulted in a very creeped-out cleaning person who left and refused to return for the rest of the evening to clean *any* rooms.

The eye team came and went, and fortunately at least bagged the body and put them on a stretcher so I could deliver them to the morgue when I got the chance. As I said, super busy trauma night, so I did not get to this task until almost 2:00 a.m. Eye team left at 10:30 p.m.

As I came off the elevator and around a corner, there stood a housekeeping girl, young lady probably in her early twenties. She looked very distraught as she asked me, "Is that a dead body?"

Not thinking about the trauma I was about to inevitably inflict upon this poor girl, I answered with a very dry serious tone, "They don't like us putting the live ones in a bag. Would you mind getting me the key to the morgue?" She shook her head dramatically to indicate no, so I asked if I could leave it with her while I go get the key, and I left her. When I returned with the key, the girl's cleaning cart was still in place, but she was nowhere to be seen.

Side note: I have never seen her again anywhere.

Insert karma: As I am backing into the morgue with the stretcher, I realize the light is off and the hair on my neck is standing up. I say to myself, "Oh, hell no," as I push the stretcher back out into the hall. I return to the room and turn all the lights on before returning to fetch the body.

Inside the morgue, there are two drawers for storage. I opened the bottom one, but it was occupied, so I opened the top one—bingo, empty!—so I slid out the tray.

At this point, I should have called for help, but I thought, *I'm a strong country girl. I can get the body in the drawer all by myself.*

I raised the stretcher to the height of the tray and began the transfer. The legs were not big, so I moved them over first. Now I never realized for some reason, just how heavy the top half of a person is when it is devoid of life. So I lifted the shoulders to move it over, and the tray, which apparently does *not* lock in the out position, slid into the drawer, leaving me between the stretcher and the drawer almost holding up the shoulders. I started to slide down because I was in too awkward of a position to move the body back to the stretcher. The body, of course, followed me to the floor and trapped me underneath it.

I will remind you at this point that the stretcher is still trapping me between it and the drawers, and now I am also trapped underneath a dead human being.

Panic sets in as I am trying everything in my power to get out, get the stretcher unlocked, roll the body to under me—anything to remove myself from this situation.

I am finally able to roll out, and in my haste, I left the body on the floor and the stretcher in the morgue. I did return the key and went back upstairs to the OR.

Upon returning, I told my charge nurse what had happened and asked if he could please call the house supervisor to let her know the body was in there and in what state it was in. He laughed for nearly thirty minutes before he pulled himself together enough to call the house supervisor.

Tripped

Nasty vascular surgeon went to sit on a chair before an AV fistula shunt insertion, tripped, contaminated himself, and tried to grab onto the sterile field, but the tech pulled the table away, and he fell on the floor—priceless!

Do You Want This on the Table?

So I'm fresh out of school and full of myself. I'm working with a fairly young doctor, and I am being a bit of an asshole to my circulating nurse. (I do not do that anymore.) She had been nasty to me on a previous occasion, so I felt justified at the time.

I keep asking for little things that I do and things that I do not need. Dumb shit like blades and pens and little stuff that I keep waiting until she sits down to ask for. Really enjoying myself asking for instruments that she has to go to the core to find. Oh, I was really having a piss, and the doc and I are really having fun with it and laughing every time she leaves the room.

Karma then rears her ugly ass, mean-spirited, spiteful, bitch of a head.

You see, I am quite short, and the hospital always seems to have gowns that are always too long for me. I just happened to be standing on a step and had my table about four feet behind me.

So the doc asks me for something that is on my table, I can't even remember what it was because what followed can only be described as Murphy getting in cahoots with karma, and the gods looking down on me and saying, "Watch this."

I step down off the step, and my toe catches the gown and pulls it straight down. The Velcro and the ties are good on this gown because it didn't even threaten to tear. So my next step, because of the momentum from the step down, just happened to be further up in the gown, due to the fact that now my head and body were headed for the floor. What happened next will go down in history as the best service of karma to hit the OR.

My arms and chest hit my table, but my foot was still pulling me down by the gown around my neck. I slid on my table because the table had decided to leave the vicinity by way of "away from me" so I pulled my whole back table to the floor with me, minus the actual table, of course.

My doctor, let's just call him Dr. Obvious from here on, looks over the patient at me lying on the floor with all of my previously sterile supplies and the fresh bottle of saline that I hadn't really needed but asked for anyway all around me and soaking through my clothes and scrub cap. He says to me, "You know you deserved that, right?"

Of course, I knew I deserved it.

My nurse returns at precisely this moment with the retractor I didn't need in her hand.

She looks at me (stifling a really hard laughter, I am sure) and says, "So do you want this on the table, or should I just hand it to you?"

Damn you, karma!

Shitatstrophe

The case started off with my preceptor saying it was a waste for me to be there. It was the surgeon's first crack at robotic colon resection and anyone's guess how well (or horribly) it would go, but I was determined to stay and learn. We took our best guess on the setup (since there was no precedent and consequently no preference card to follow).

With the robot and patient draped and ready, we waited for the doctor (Dr. A) and *her* assistant, a fellow surgeon (Dr. B), alpha male, to arrive.

We were doomed from the start. Everything from the placement of ports to docking the robot, and which instruments to use was an argument between the two surgeons. Dr. A wanted to use a PK forceps; Dr. B argued that a fenestrated grasper was better to take down the omentum. If Dr. B wanted to take down the omentum, Dr. A argued that they should search for the area to resect instead. Technically it was Dr. A's case, but you'd never know it listening to the quarrel. Dr. B, a particularly obstinate individual, began then to pick apart everything Dr. A did.

Dr. A wasn't dissecting in the right plane.

Dr. A wasn't dissecting fast enough.

Dr. A wasn't approaching the resection from the right direction.

Over several hours, the situation deteriorated into Dr. A with Dr. B to abort the robotic approach and switch to a more typical laparoscopic one, Dr. B simultaneously refusing to give up on the robot and berating Dr. A and everyone in the room for every minor infraction, from not handing instruments fast enough to the volume of the music.

I was finally relieved for lunch.

When I returned, the relief tech met me in the sub-sterile room. He looked exhausted. Like he had aged fifteen years in the thirty minutes I had been gone. I asked how things were going, and he just shook his head, saying, "Good luck," as he drifted, shell-shocked down the hallway.

While I had been gone, Dr. A had finally won, and they had abandoned the use of the robot. Dr. B had conceded using the robot but continued his verbal assault as they finally removed the offending section of bowel.

It had been nearly six hours at this point, and I was elated that this nightmare of a surgery was close to an end. They finished the anastomosis then proceeded to do a round of rock, paper, scissors to determine who was going "downstairs" (to the anus) to pump air in and check for leaks. Dr. B (the obstinate one) lost, and despite being near people's buttholes being a normal part of their day, I secretly reveled in his loss.

Dr. B pumped in the air while we filled the abdomen with saline to watch for bubbles, indicating a leak in the anastomosis. By some divine intervention, there was none. The saline was suctioned out of the abdomen, and Dr. A began pressing down the bowel to release air from the bowel.

At this moment, Karma decided to rear its ugly head. As Dr. A was pressing down, a stream of curse words erupted from Dr. B. I looked down just in time to see the stream of curse words accompanied by an eruption of excrement from the patient's bowels, aimed directly at Dr. B.

(At this point, I would like to say that I have seen patients poop intraoperatively. In surgery, poop happens, literally. It's not a huge deal; you just clean it up and move on. Not this time; there was no moving on. Okay, now back to our story.)

The literal poop-storm hit Dr. B squarely in the chest. I thought after the first hit that it would stop, but the deluge of dung kept coming, and Dr. B, still in shock, made no attempt to dodge the mess. My second thought after *Oh my god, that's a lot of poo* was *This could not have happened to a more deserving individual.* Dr. A was relishing the moment of karmic revenge but finally took pity on the now sodden Dr. B. She looked down at his misery and said, "Oh sorry, maybe I should stop pushing."

Dr. B was *pissed!* He stripped off his gown and gloves and stormed from the room, presumably to hose off somewhere (hopefully outdoors). No sooner had Dr. B left than the entire room erupted into a riotous laughter. The tension of the previous six hours evaporated, and we finished the case feeling strangely relieved and slightly vindicated.

The account of our room's exploits, along with the horrible smell, spread throughout the entire OR well before we finished closing.

I won't lie—after the humor of the situation had worn off, the aftermath of the shitastrophe wasn't pretty. The room was so contaminated that the case set to follow had to be rescheduled, and it took an army of OR employees cleaning the room just to get the stink to dissipate from the adjacent hallways.

It has only been a few months since this happened, but the "epic robotic poop case" is already well known throughout the OR. Was the epic awfulness of the entire encounter worth it? Heck yeah!

I have worked with Dr. B several times since, and apparently the experience made an impact. He has been perfectly lovely and helpful ever since that day. So I guess the moral of the story is, "Don't give people shit if you can't take it, because sooner or later…karma." Or maybe the moral of the story is, "Assholes come in all shapes and sizes, but the worst ones are those that spew crap." I haven't decided, but in either case, always wear eyewear and an impervious gown, because you never know when shit will happen, kids.

Nope

I was early in my career working at a teaching hospital with an endless rotation of new surgical residents and medical students. We had a patient in jackknife position for a hemorrhoidectomy, cheeks taped and prepped, when he proceeded to have projectile diarrhea that shot across the room and all over the cabinet behind him. The new resident turned to me while I was conferring with the scrub tech and said, "You gonna clean that up?" I told him where the towels were and that he could help himself.

It's Gonna Blow

During an exploratory laparotomy, the doctor was milking the bowel to decompress. I could see that the bowel was getting very distended south of where he was looking.

I barely had time to shout "It's gonna—" and before I could get out the word *blow* out of my mouth, that distended bowel exploded like a volcanic eruption. I said "*Shit.*"

The doctor looked down at me and said, "Yep, it is" (as I was covered head-to-toe with it). Yuck 🙂. Pretty sure I heard some sniggering going on underneath that mask.

Cut Me

Dragged through the Mud

Also TN… Had a guy who worked in a fish-processing business. Stepped on a catfish barb, pierced bottom of foot. He came in for I&D. He didn't follow instructions post-op, went to a demolition derby, got in a fight with his baby momma's new boyfriend, and his dressing was torn off and the foot dragged through mud. Came back multiple times and finally ended up with AKA. I wish I could share his name, because it is absolutely the icing on the cake

Item Received in Damaged Condition

Once had a patient for a repeat rectal procedure. The patient was a postal worker. As they were drifting off to sleep, they stated, "I hope you all have a sense of humor." As we positioned them in jackknife, a sticker became visible: "Item received in damaged condition." Laughter ensued.

Is This Eight Inches to You?

Surgeon, hand out: Eight-inch peon.

(Me: hands him said clamp)

Surgeon (looks, hands it back): "I said 8 inches"
Me (grabs the biggest clamp I can find): "Is this 8 inches to you?"
Surgeon (luckily laughs): I deserved that

Asshat

Had a surgeon ready to cement the total shoulder stem when the suction clogged. Scrub nurse was trying to unclog with a syringe right as the surgeon was taking it apart, and it exploded. The surgeon was covered, and he could get back to getting the stem cemented while cement was ready. Once he got it in, he stepped back, put his head down, shaking it in defeat. I said, "What's wrong now?" and he said, "I was just recounting what just happened."

Might not be the funniest story, but he was and is an asshat, so it makes me happy every time I think of it. 😊

Statements Commonly Heard in the OR

"Who put the foley in the patient's...?!!" 🌀

How aggressively I pass instruments *does* have a direct correlation to your attitude.

Get under my gown and get it.

Can someone tie me up?

I just need a knife and some suture!

It's only going to take an hour!

Wipe the tip!

That's what she said!

You do realize I am handing you ALL of the sharp shit, right?

All bleeding will stop eventually.

Man, you pass out one time holding a penis and you can never live it down.

I tripped and fell on it, in the shower.

GLOSSARY OF TERMS

AKA. Not "also known as"! At least you still have an ass.

Andrews table. Not Mary's table.

anterior. If you are looking at the patient's ass, flip them over.

aorta bifem. You are having a bad day.

AWOL. They are not where they are supposed to be. Hiding, I suppose. Check the PACU lounge.

barfed. Renting a meal.

Bovie. Hot stick.

CABG. Not lettuce.

C-arm. Comes after A-arm and B-arm.

cautery. What the hot stick does.

chloraprep. Fake suntan.

chole. Bag that holds nasty shit.

circulator. Not your mom.

colectomy. Taking the color out of the colon.

crani. What we're gonna do is, we are going to saw the top of your head off.

CRNA. The candy will not crush itself.

CST. Instrument slinger.

cysto. Splash zone.

D&C. Get in there, scrape it, and suck it.

ED. Where you don't want to be during a full moon.

ENT. Booger picker.

extubation/intubation. Shoving the tube down the throat and sometimes the patient ripping it out.

FA. Glorifies surgical tech.

Foley. Pee-pee tube.

forceps. Grabbies.

gastroscopic. Looking at your meal after you ate it.

GI tech. Masters of Brown Town.

GU. Yellow brick road.

hernia. Clearly not as strong as you thought.

hover mat. The equalizer.

hydrocele. Not an actual animal in the water.

ICU. No, you do not.

impaction. What happens when you go in the out door.

inject. Using the stabby thing to shove fluid into the body.

lap. Not once around the track.

lipoma. Big fat ball of hardened fat.

lithotomy. Get those legs in the air.

loogie. Snot rocket.

MAC. Sarcastic name for a stranger.

megacolon. Not a little one.

MF. Exactly what you think it means.

mucus plug. Slimy baby stopper. Also can stop other things.

murse. Nurse you have to ask for things in multiple times. Not a female.

NP. The brains behind the doctor.

OB-GYN. The doctor that catches the baby.

OCD. The person that is easiest to mess with.

omentum. Cushion to colon.

ORIF. Cut it open and slap some screws and/or plates on it.

PA. Surgeon's right hand.

PACU. The place you think you kind of remember, but you think it might have been a dream.

Penrose drain. Rubber thingy.

perfed. Poked a hole in it.

pessary. Device used to keep the bladder from falling out of the vagina.

PID. Ouchy, itchy hoo-haw.

post-partem. After the miracle, before they know everything.

prep. Get ready.

prolapse. When it falls out.

prostatectomy. Pop out the prostate.

prosthetic. Not real.

rep. The one who holds the surgeon's hand.
RN. The real knowledge in the room.
SCDs. Have nothing to do with sexual activity.
scrub sink. Where you do the washy thing.
sedate. Removal of annoyances.
shaft. I think you know this.
SPD. Where the instruments go to get ready for the next show.
sphincter. Not just your butthole.
SSI. Hospital bugs.
STD. If you don't know by now, I can't help you.
tech. The specialist.
TLIF. The long way around to the spine.
trach. The hole in your neck that you smoke through.
urologist. The doctor that looks at your junk.
Versed. Amnesia juice.

ABOUT THE AUTHOR

Deanne has been a surgical tech for thirteen years. She has experienced a wealth of trauma and has been present for a lot of happy and sad moments in her time in the OR.

www.ingramcontent.com/pod-product-compliance
Lightning Source LLC
Chambersburg PA
CBHW031424150726
47989CB00002B/788